ST MARTIN'S
TRUE CRIME CLASSICS

D1213691

"Who's there?"

Herb flipped on the porch light and peered out the door's peephole. He saw a young girl with a bent head. He opened the door to a horrifying sight. The girl's clothes were saturated with blood. She swayed in the glow of the porch light.

He opened the door and led her into the still-dark house. "Marlene, take care of this little girl. I need to call 9-1-1."

Marlene stood in the doorway of the bedroom. She switched on the kitchen light. An intense image of red branded itself on the surface of Marlene's eyes. "My God. My God. What happened to you?"

For a second, Herb froze, unable to remember how to dial 9-1-1. Then he stabbed in the numbers. As soon as he heard the answering click, he blurted, "I have a little girl . . ." He glanced at the pathetic form desperately clinging to life. He thought of his own grandchildren. He could not utter the word "dying." "She's covered in blood. I need an ambulance. I need police. Please hurry."

Krystal mimed a writing pen. Marlene stepped into the kitchen area for a pen and pad of paper. Herb hung up the phone.

Marlene handed the pen and paper to Krystal. Herb knelt by her side. He held her hand. He stroked her hair, trying to get it out of the blood caked on her face.

The young girl scrawled: "The Harrises are hurt."

"Who did this to you?"

"This guy," scratched across the paper . . .

THROUGH
THE WINDOW

*To Karen —
The Queen of Justice!*

DIANE FANNING

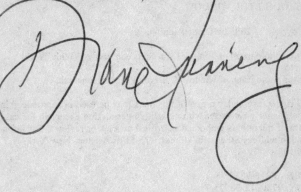

St. Martin's Paperbacks

THROUGH THE WINDOW

Copyright © 2003 by Diane Fanning.

Cover photograph of Tommy Lynn Sells courtesy AP/Wide World Photos.
Cover photograph of window © Steven Puetzer/Nonstock.

ISBN: 0-312-98525-8
EAN: 9780312-98525-7

Printed in the United States of America

St. Martin's Paperbacks edition / April 2003

10 9 8 7 6 5

This book is dedicated to two heroic survivors,
Krystal Surles and Fabienne Witherspoon;
to Kaylene Harris, who made the final sacrifice;
and to all the known and unknown victims who preceded her.

ACKNOWLEDGMENTS

FOLLOWING the trail of crimes left by Tommy Lynn Sells was a complicated and sometimes contradictory journey. I intruded on the busy days of numerous members of law enforcement along the way. More often than not, I spoke with investigators with technically open cases who were restricted in the information they could impart. Nonetheless, this situation did not inhibit their generosity with their time.

Thanks to: Lt. Terry Ward, Little Rock, Arkansas; Detective Jeffrey Stone, St. Louis; Don Swann, Taney County, Missouri; Mike Curti, former Winnemucca Police Chief, and James Bagwell, former Humboldt County Sheriff, in Nevada; Detective Karen Wright, Tucson; Lt. Richard Podgers, Lockport, New York; Detective John Kemp, Jefferson County, Illinois; Capt. Diana Sievers, Illinois State Police; Investigator Donny Branch, Jackson County, Florida; Sgt. Rick Westfall, Charleston, West Virginia; Detective Sgt. Jim Arnott, Greene County, Missouri; Sgt. Buddy Cooper, Missouri Highway Patrol; Lt. Jimmy Hand, Gibson County, Tennessee; Detective Chris Schoonover, Lexington, Kentucky; Agent Steve Tanio and Public Information Officer Kym Koch, Oklahoma State Bureau of Investigation; and Lt. Larry Pope, Val Verde, Texas. A very special thanks to my two favorite lawmen, for whom I have the greatest respect for their dedication, tenacity and commitment, Texas Rangers Sgt. John Allen and Sgt. Coy Smith.

On the legal side, many thanks to Prosecuting Attorney Jim Kopp, Bexar County, Texas; Assistant District Attorney Ard Gates, Kingfisher County, Oklahoma; State's

Attorney Gary Duncan, Jefferson County, Illinois; Prosecuting Attorney Rodney Daniels, Taney County, Missouri; Mary Anne Wiley in Governor Perry's policy office in Texas; retired Judge George M. Thurmond, Val Verde County, Texas; Diana Hancock, Texas Court of Criminal Appeals; Brenda Loudermilk, Attorney General's Office in Austin, Texas; and Larry Fitzgerald, Texas Department of Criminal Justice. And lots of appreciation to the private sector attorneys who helped me to understand the wranglings of the law: Larry Sauer and Will Harrell in Austin and Ron Friesenhahn in New Braunfels.

Others who provided invaluable assistance in my research were Jeff Marcinik of the Humboldt County Public Library in Winnemucca, Nevada; Larry Sonntag, M.S., LPC-CCDS in New Braunfels; Iris Taber in Dallas; JoAnn Settle in Ina, Illinois: Fernando Perez and Noel Sanchez in San Antonio; Herb and Marlene Betz in Del Rio; Jenna Jackson, producer for *48 Hours*; Claire J. Weinraub, producer for *20/20*; Scott Fulmer of Investigations Across Missouri; and friend, former neighbor and top-notch investigator, Dan Phillips of Mission Investigations of Dallas, Houston, San Antonio, the Rio Grande Valley and Louisiana.

Thanks to Tommy Lynn Sells for hours of interviews, prolific correspondence and a mountain of legal documents. And thanks to his mother, Nina Sells, his great aunt Bonnie Walpole, and his mother-in-law, Virginia Blanco.

A compassionate acknowledgment of my gratitude to the family members of victims, who allowed me a glimpse into the blackest moments of their lives: Crystal Harris, Kathleen Cowling, Anna Walker, Joni Settlemeir, Joeann Dardeen, Anita Knapp, Inez Cowling, Pamela Surles, Lorene Bible and Susan Wofford. I will never forget you.

On a personal note, I want to thank writer Suzy Spencer, my mentor, cheerleader and gentle critic for putting her hands behind my back and giving me a shove.

To David Ferguson, News Editor of KNBT–KGNB radio in New Braunfels—thanks for pumping up the jam.

To Wayne—I would never have persevered without

your unending emotional support, toleration and love.

And, finally, I must honor my huge debt of gratitude to the three people who made this book possible: my agent, Jane Dystel; St. Martin's Press executive editor, Charlie Spicer; and the man with the scrupulous eye, my editor, Joe Cleeman.

CHAPTER ONE

A chill teased the air across South Texas in the early morning hours of December 31, 1999. In less than twenty hours, thousands would light fireworks to herald the coming of a new century, the promise of a new beginning. Just west of Del Rio, on the Guajia Bay, nothing so remarkable heralded the departure of one young life and the end of innocence for another.

Down a dark, narrow road, the six inhabitants of a double-wide mobile home were fast asleep at 4:30 A.M. The man outside the residence first tried to trip the lock on the back door with his knife blade, but failed. The family dog started barking in the pen. He let the black rottweiler smell his hand and patted him on the head until the animal was quiet. He removed the screen from the window above the air conditioner and pushed up on the sash, but the latch lock was drawn, holding the pane in place.

He moved on panther feet to the front of the house. The window to 14-year-old Justin Harris' room was raised to the welcome coolness of a mild December. Outside, the open window was an invitation to the man lurking in the shadows. He removed that screen and set it off to the side. Beneath his makeshift entryway, a large metal tub rested. He stepped up on its edge, unaware that in the dark water below his foot, two ill-tempered snapping turtles waited for him to slip. From his perch, he pushed the sash up a bit farther until he created an opening large enough for entry. Carefully, he threw one leg up over the windowsill and into the room. He paused, his ears tuned to catch the slightest noise. He hoisted the other leg into the room and eased himself down to the floor.

Justin, blind from birth, thought one of the girls was messing with him again, and said, "Will you all stop coming into my room?" then went back to sleep.

The intruder walked into the next bedroom and struck his lighter. There was a very small girl sleeping on the bed, 7-year-old Marque Surles. Her heart-shaped face looked even more innocent in repose than it did by day—nose smooshed in the pillow, delicate eyelashes feathered on its case. Her body curled up in a loose, comfortable ball. He stared at her in the flickering light. Then, he turned away.

He walked down the hall to the other end of the trailer. Spinning the ridged wheel on his lighter again, he saw a woman, Crystal Harris, and a young girl, 12-year-old Lori Harris, fast asleep. He touched the woman on the leg. She did not stir. He looked down at her long hair splayed across the pillow, at the curves of her body undulating beneath the covers. He shook his head and stepped away.

He went back down the hall to explore the one remaining bedroom. Stepping across the threshold, all he heard was the quiet flow of breath from the two occupants in the room. He inhaled a heady smell: part sweaty child, part air freshener, part blooming female adolescence.

He pulled the door closed behind him. In the top bunk, 10-year-old Krystal Surles stirred, and he froze in his tracks. No thread of light penetrated the room. He was unable to identify the source of the noise. His right hand squeezed the knife handle until it left a deep impression on his palm. In two steps, he was leaning over 13-year-old Kaylene "Katy" Harris on the lower level of the bed. "Wake up," he hissed into her ear. He lay down next to her and held one hand to her trembling throat while his other hand wielded a hideous twelve-inch boning knife.

"What are *you* doing here?"

Without responding, he slit her shorts. He cut her panties. He sliced her bra in two. Then he returned the knife to the terrified child's throat while his free hand danced across her small body. She jerked free, tumbling out of bed on the side that was closest to the wall.

She shouted, "Go get Mama!" as she surged toward the door. But he was already there blocking her escape. His knife stabbed, drawing first blood.

"Look, you cut me."

He flipped on the light and looked at the fresh wound on her arm, and pulled her toward him. Above, Krystal awoke with a start, peering through the slats of the bunk. First she saw Katy; a hairy hand was clasped over her friend's mouth. Then, her worst nightmare came true: she saw him—the monster under the bed lived! He stood behind Katy, holding a wicked-looking knife to her throat. As the 13-year-old struggled, Krystal looked in her eyes. She received an urgent message that was as loud and clear as if spoken: "Do not move."

Without warning, the knife sliced. A helpless Krystal watched as a long red streak of blood raced across Katy's neck. The knife pulled back and cut again, deepening the wound. The 13-year-old twisted away, clutched at a poster on the wall and pulled it down with her. She fell to the floor, gagging, choking, gasping for air as she drowned in a profusion of her own blood. He leaned over her, stabbing her stomach, her chest, her arms until he was certain he had completed what he had begun.

The intruder then turned to the top bunk where he saw Krystal for the first time.

"I'll be quiet. I promise. I won't say nothing. I'm not making a noise. It's Katy, not me," she begged.

In response, the silent stranger brought the menacing knife toward her throat. Her jerking hands flew up to that vulnerable part of her small eighty-pound frame in a valiant attempt to defend it from assault. "Please don't hurt me," she whimpered.

He answered her pathetic plea with a cold command: "Move your hands." When she did not comply, he brushed them away and brought the boning knife across her throat with sufficient violence to slice her windpipe in two. Krystal uttered not a sound. She lay motionless, smelling the acrid scent of blood and the pungent odor of her own fear. She fought back the urge to flee, instinct warning her that any sign of life would ensure instant death. The bearded, long-haired nightmare turned off the bedroom lights and left the room.

Still, Krystal did not move. Her heart pounded with anxiety, dreading that the man would return. When she could bear it no longer, she got out of the bed on the side next to the wall. She pushed on the window there, but could not open it. Feeling her way with her hands, she moved to the end of the bed, identified her suitcase by touch and stumbled over the limp, bloody body of her best friend. Without thinking, Krystal lay down next to her. She patted the other girl's leg with pitiful tenderness, hoping she could make the horrible noises stop. Katy showed no sign of receiving the comfort her desperate friend wanted to impart. Her body, ravaged by sixteen stab wounds and two severe lacerations, was unable to respond.

Krystal thought she heard a car start and drive away in the distance. She felt her way to the bedroom door, banging her toes hard into the ladder to the bunk bed that had fallen in her path. She moved it out of the way and exited the room. Help was just down the hall, but she did not know it. Her thoughts were consumed by brilliant images of red and the gut-wrenching sounds of a dying friend. Believing her attacker had killed everyone else in the house, she fled the horror, out into the naked night.

CHAPTER TWO

A quarter-mile down the desolate road, Herb Betz woke to his alarm clock at 4:45 A.M. He'd planned to get up early and watch the first New Year's celebration of the millennium live from New Zealand at 5. He awoke, changed his mind, switched off his alarm and went back to sleep.

Outside, in plaid boxers, a tee shirt and socks, Krystal stumbled down the narrow tar-and-gravel road. There were no streetlights. There was no moon. The road dipped and turned through rough countryside covered in cactus and stunted shrubs, inhabited by snakes, rabbits, tarantulas and scorpions.

She stepped onto the front porch of the nearest trailer. Then she remembered that Terry Harris had had a dispute with this neighbor and ordered them all not to go to that home.

She turned around without knocking and trudged farther up the road to the white trailer with green and brown trim, the home of Herb and Marlene Betz. She pressed the cranky, unreliable doorbell and waited. Her knees wobbled. Her head spun. Her train of thought had only one refrain: "Please, God, don't let me die. Please, God, don't let me die." Herb glanced at the clock. It was 4:58 A.M. He pulled on a pair of pants, wondering who could be at his door at this hour. Krystal leaned on the button again. By the time Herb reached the front door, the pounding of a knocking fist echoed through the trailer.

"Who's there?"

She tried to speak. Impossible. Tears of frustration and

fear pooled in her eyes. She wanted to scream. Instead, she fell on the doorbell again.

Herb flipped on the porch light and peered out the door's peephole. He saw a young girl with a bent head. He opened the door to a horrifying sight. Krystal raised her chin and pointed to her throat. He saw both ends of her severed windpipe protruding from her neck. A thick clot of blood, more than three inches wide, was hanging from her gaping wound to the middle of her chest. Her clothes were saturated with blood. She swayed in the glow of the porch light.

He opened the door and led her into the still-dark house. "Marlene, take care of this little girl. I need to call 9-1-1."

Marlene stood in the doorway of the bedroom. She switched on the kitchen light. An intense image of red branded itself on the surface of Marlene's eyes. "My God. My God. What happened to you?"

For a second, Herb froze, unable to remember how to dial 9-1-1. Then he stabbed in the numbers. As soon as he heard the answering click, he blurted, "I have a little girl . . ." He glanced at the pathetic form desperately clinging to life. He thought of his own grandchildren. He could not utter the word "dying." "She's covered in blood. I need an ambulance. I need police. Please hurry."

Krystal mimed a writing pen. Marlene stepped into the kitchen area for a pen and pad of paper. Herb hung up the phone.

When they both turned back to Krystal, she had lain down on the kitchen floor. She told them later that she was worried she would get blood on their "nice carpet."

Marlene handed the pen and paper to Krystal. Herb knelt by her side. He held her hand. He stroked her hair, trying to get it out of the blood caked on her face.

The young girl scrawled: "The Harrises are hurt."

"An ambulance is coming," Herb responded.

"Where do you live?" Marlene asked.

"Kansas," she wrote.

"Who did this to you?"

"This guy," scratched across the paper.

Marlene wanted to ask more, but stopped. Krystal looked so frail, so close to death.

The phone rang and Marlene grabbed it, giving directions to the dispatcher.

Krystal wrote, "Tell them to hurry."

Still on the phone, Marlene relayed a message to Herb. "They say you need to stop the bleeding."

He pulled a kitchen towel out of a drawer and moved it toward Krystal's throat. Showing the first break in her calm demeanor, Krystal frantically waved it away. She knew the towel would cover her windpipe and cut off her only supply of air.

Marlene hung up the phone and opened the blinds on the window facing out to the lake and to the highway. Just then, an ambulance and a sheriff's vehicle raced past their turnoff, lights flashing, sirens shrieking.

Marlene jerked the phone off the wall and dialed 9-1-1. "Tell them to turn around. They drove right by."

The dispatcher told her to go out to the highway and flag them down. Marlene knew she could never get out that far in time. So, she picked up the flashlight and, standing on the porch, streaked its beam across the sky. She swung it back and forth, until she saw the emergency vehicles race past in the opposite direction, back up, then turn off and drive through the stone arch leading to Guajia Bay.

Krystal wrote, "Will I live?"

Herb bent down, kissed her on the forehead and said, "Everything will be all right." But he did not believe it. He felt certain that he was watching her die on his vinyl floor. He turned away to hide his tears. Krystal's body began shaking with escalating violence.

AT 5:12 A.M., the wailing whine of the approaching sirens halted at the Betzes' door. Emergency medical personnel entered first, racing to the side of the wounded child. Deputies Manuel Pena and Ramiro Reyes were right on their heels. They were not prepared for what they found. They'd thought dispatcher Jim Saavedra had sent them to the Betz home in reference to a young girl involved in a motor vehicle accident. The girl was reported to have a cut in her neck area. It was a far more traumatic wound than they had anticipated.

After talking to paramedic Lori Martinez, the deputies told the dispatcher that the girl was bleeding very heavily and was going into convulsions. "There is a cut to the front of her neck and a lot of blood on her shirt and on the floor of the kitchen."

Herb took the deputies out on his porch and, pointing to the Harris home, told them that more people were hurt there. The night was so dark, the house on the hill was not visible. The men jumped into their car and drove off to face the unknown a quarter mile away.

The emergency medical attendants attempted to insert a trach down Krystal's throat, but she gagged and was unable to breathe. They stabilized her as best they could and loaded her into the ambulance.

A courageous child clutched at a tenuous thread of life as she was whisked to the heliport at the local hospital and airlifted to University Hospital in San Antonio.

CHAPTER THREE

AT the Harris home, Pena and Reyes explored the perimeter of the double-wide trailer overlooking Lake Amistad. They avoided the growling rottweiler, but gave even wider berth to the fenced-in alligator in the backyard. They noted a damaged window blind, and that the front door was ajar eight to ten inches.

Del Rio police officers Fred Knoll and Charles Saints, their back-up, arrived, and the four men entered, opening the screen door and carefully pushing the unlocked front door open. Shining their flashlights inside, they saw living room walls decorated with African weapons and masks. In the kitchen beyond, festive Christmas accessories sparkled in the beam of the searching lights. Reyes shouted, "Sheriff's office!" three times.

Within seconds, Crystal Harris and her daughter, Lori, emerged from the west-end bedroom to confront the men in her home. Simultaneously, Pena and Reyes fired a question at her.

"Is everyone okay?"

"Is anyone on the east side of the residence?"

Pointing toward that end of the house, Crystal said, "My other daughter is in her room. What's going on?" Tears streamed down her face.

Deputies Pena and Reyes and Officer Saints left the living room to search the home. Officer Knoll remained there attempting to calm Crystal, but she demanded answers that he just did not have. She protectively clutched Lori to her side and mindlessly ran her hands over her daughter's hair. The tension etched furrows in her face.

• • •

WHEN Pena turned on the light in Katy's bedroom, they saw her sprawled on the floor. Blood oozed from her lifeless form. Brilliant red spatter covered all four walls. Stains marred the bedding and etched themselves into the frame on both the upper and lower bunks of the bed.

Katy was nude from the waist down. The cut in her neck gaped and her windpipe stuck out obscenely. Her pink shorts and panties lay on the floor by the door. Deputy Pena could not find a pulse. Officer Saints checked, too, ruefully shaking his head at his failure to find one.

Checking another room, they found Justin, Crystal's blind son. The perpetrator had entered this house through the open window in his room. Justin was unharmed.

In the next bedroom, they found 7-year-old Marque Surles, adrift in bliss, unaware of the fragility of her life that night.

When the officers stepped across the threshold of the master bedroom door, they heard stealthy sounds of movement. Their hands automatically hefted their guns. Carefully, one arm stretched toward the light switch, flicked it on and revealed the secrets of the room. All six eyes riveted on the source of the noise—a small zoo of caged snakes, including a few rattlesnakes whose raised tails now added back-up percussion to the sandpaper slither of many coiling bodies. Keeping their distance from the reptiles, they checked the room thoroughly, finding no one.

They sealed Katy's bedroom and called dispatch to request the presence of Lieutenants Skelton, Pope and Sunderland. Pena reported, "I've got a DOA, and need a justice of the peace, too."

EMS attendants Dexter Tooke, Susie Jo Chow and Jack Howley raced into the house and checked on Katy. Dexter cut her shirt to attach three pads with leads to monitor her heart. It was a useless attempt.

Hearing the activity on the scanner, Texas Ranger

Johnny Allen called Pope and offered his assistance. Pope told him that he wasn't exactly sure what he had on his hands, but he'd be glad to have some help.

CRYSTAL, Lori and Justin were escorted from the house and into patrol units outside. Little Marque Surles was left in bed asleep, dreaming sweet dreams while she still could.

After he arrived, Ranger Allen called for a DPS crime-scene team. Then, he sat next to Crystal in the back of the cruiser and asked her the most sensitive and worrisome question on their minds: "Where is your husband, Terry Harris?"

Crystal answered without hesitation. He'd left Del Rio about 6 P.M. on December 30 with Shawn Harris, his son from a previous marriage, along with Doug Luker, Pam Surles' boyfriend, and his two sons, Jarrett and Matthew. They had traveled to Kansas to help Pam pack and move to Del Rio.

Pope reached Terry Harris on his cell phone. After asking where he was, he instructed Harris to proceed to the nearest law enforcement office. When he did, Harris' location in Kansas was confirmed. Doubt was raised about their first suspicions, and they had no clue of where to look next.

The investigators protected the exterior of the scene and waited for the forensic specialists to arrive. After a few hours, a team consisting of a photographer, a person responsible for trace evidence, an individual assigned to DNA and a latent print examiner arrived on the scene. They gathered evidence that day until after dark.

When they had finished, Deputy Larry Stamps called the funeral home. They transported Katy Harris to the autopsy table in San Antonio. Krystal Surles was already in the San Antonio hospital, desperately clinging to life. Against all odds, doctors there struggled to prevent her from joining her friend.

CHAPTER FOUR

Upon arrival at University Hospital, Krystal was rushed into surgery. The knife wound had nicked the sheath on her carotid artery, but the artery itself was uncut. Del Rio medical personnel had intubated her prior to her arrival in San Antonio. Now, the most urgent task for the staff here was to maintain her airway. Massive swelling and distortion in the area complicated their objective. Untreated, this swelling would have caused her to suffocate slowly.

Their second concern was the blood draining into her lungs. Although the five-inch slice spared her carotid artery, it did sever many other vessels in the area. She could have drowned in her own blood from this seepage.

Finally, they labored to repair her severed larynx. They had saved her life, but would not know for days whether their efforts had been completely successful—they would not know until little Krystal could talk again.

At 5 A.M. on New Year's Day, Allen and Pope left Del Rio. Texas Ranger Coy Smith from Uvalde joined them in San Antonio. At the side of Dr. Jan Garavaglia, they viewed the autopsy of Katy Harris at the Bexar County Forensic Center. Her carotid artery had been severed, as had her jugular vein. The wound to her neck went all the way down to her vertebrae. In addition to having her throat cut, she had suffered sixteen stab wounds—three of them going all the way through her body and exiting on the other side.

The moment she regained consciousness, 10-year-old Krystal sought justice. Determined to put her attacker behind bars, her hands and arms scribed stubborn, nearly violent gestures in the air to indicate her demand for a pen and paper.

A call came from the hospital to the forensic center. Dr. Cynthia Beamer informed Val Verde Sheriff's Department Lieutenant Larry Pope, "Krystal wants to talk."

"Krystal's talking?"

"No, she's writing." And she wanted investigators there right away.

POPE and Allen rushed to University Hospital. In the intensive care unit, they attempted to gently ease their young witness into the questioning about the night's events. Krystal would have none of that—she wanted to get straight to the point, scrawling out vivid details on her notepad. She started writing with her right hand, then she shifted to her left—forming words as easily with one hand as with the other.

She had seen her attacker and remembered what he looked like. Unbelievable, the two men thought. Ranger Allen grabbed a telephone and called the Department of Public Safety's forensic artist, Shirley Timmons, at her home in Midland. Without hesitation, she cut her holiday weekend short, grabbed her supplies and flew down to San Antonio.

KRYSTAL'S mother, Pam, was at her daughter's side as the girl communicated the harrowing experience. Pam and Doug Luker had driven thirteen hours from Kansas to the hospital the day before, arriving just in time to ring in the New Year. Before the artist arrived, the investigators asked Luker about a likely suspect. Krystal's written description reminded him of a man he and Terry Harris had talked to at the convenience store next to Ram Country on the evening they left for Kansas.

AFTER introducing Shirley Timmons and Krystal Surles, the investigators left the two alone. Timmons' work was interrupted by the young girl's exhaustion. She would drift

into a short nap, then wake and work with the artist again.
When they were finished, they had a detailed drawing of
the bearded, long-haired man in question.

By this time, Luker was nearly in Del Rio. Contacting
him by cell phone, Allen made arrangements to meet him
in Uvalde. When shown the artist sketch, he was certain
the drawing looked like the man they had seen at the Pico
Convenience Store parking lot as they prepared to leave
town on December 30. He thought that the man's name
was Tom or Tommy and that he worked at Amigo Auto
Sales.

From the Uvalde DPS office, Ranger Allen called Bill
Hughes, the owner of the dealership. Hughes would not
give him a name. As soon as he hung up the phone, though,
Hughes dialed the number for the Val Verde County Sher-
iff's Department and talked to Sheriff D'Wayne Jernigan.
"The man you're looking for," he said, "is Tommy Lynn
Sells."

At the same time, Terry Harris was driving around Del
Rio in his pick-up truck with a rifle by his side. Vowing
revenge, he told all who would listen that he was going to
kill the man who'd murdered his adopted daughter, Katy.
Many believe without doubt that he'd known all along who
that man was. Yet, he would tell the name to no one. And
although he knew where the man lived, he never confronted
him at his home.

ONCE Sheriff Jernigan gave them a name, Texas Rangers
needed a six-pack of driver's license photos to lay down
for Krystal. Ranger Coy Smith was now at the hospital,
too. He hated to disturb the DPS analyst, Alice Buchanon,
at night on a holiday weekend, but he placed the call. Like
Timmons, Buchanon did not hesitate for a moment. Reluctant to make the trip alone, she swung by and picked up
her daughter to give her company on the more-than-fifty-
mile drive from Thorndale to the headquarters in Austin.

At headquarters, she faced an additional challenge. It
was January 1, 2000, and Y2K concerns permeated nearly

every office in America—the Texas Department of Public Safety was no exception. The entire computer system had been shut down as a safety precaution. Buchanon fired up the computers, hoped for the best and performed the state agency's first post-Y2K system check.

In short time, she had the photos ready for San Antonio. The only shot she found of Tommy Lynn Sells was beardless. It would have to do. Austin-based Texas Ranger Jim Denman rushed the line-up down seventy-five miles of interstate 35 to the DPS office in San Antonio where he was met by Rangers Allen and Smith.

ALLEN and Pope laid the photo spread of six beardless men in front of their young survivor. She studied each photo, her brow furrowed, her eyes intense. Then, when she had completed her survey, she prodded the photo of Tommy Lynn Sells.

At that revelation, Allen and Pope wanted to caper around the hospital room, exchanging high fives. Instead, they maintained professional composure, not giving Krystal the slightest signal. They asked her again to look at the pictures and be certain she'd picked the right man.

Her chin jutted out like the prow of a boat. She slammed her finger into Sells' picture and glared at the officers. When questioned again, she pounded her finger into the photo again. And again. And again. Krystal Surles had no doubts. The I.D. was positive.

CHAPTER FIVE

EVERY member of law enforcement in Del Rio was on high alert. Edginess sometimes overcame good police procedure. Deputy Larry Stamps prowled the streets and the back roads of the surrounding countryside looking for anything suspicious. At one trailer, he thought he saw someone— maybe Tommy Lynn Sells—lurking outside a window. Inside the home, a slumber party for a group of young girls was in full swing. Stamps pulled his gun and crept around the perimeter. When he turned the final corner, he looked straight into the barrels of a shotgun and sweated at the sound of a cocked lever.

The homeowner was taking no chances. Hearing stealthy movements outside, he was prepared. He did not lower his sights until he was convinced of Stamps' official identity.

Meanwhile, serious preparations for the apprehension of Tommy Lynn Sells proceeded. He was located five miles from the Harris house in a trailer at the American Campgrounds and Mobile Park where he lived with his wife, Jessica, and his stepchildren.

Before six A.M., on January 2, 2000, law enforcement surrounded the modest home. In the early morning hours, they assumed their positions quietly—but not quietly enough for the dogs tied in front of the house. Sells stepped out on the front porch to hush them.

Lieutenant Pope and Deputy Stamps met Sells at his front door. "Have you been having trouble with your mother-in-law?" Pope asked. "Well, I got a call, same old thing—bitching and complaining. Can I come in and talk to you?"

Sells held the door open. Once inside, Pope said, "I'm placing you under arrest. Turn around and put your hands on the counter." Sells complied without argument as he was frisked and cuffed. He was no stranger to the procedure. Pope asked him if he knew why they were there.

"No," he answered.

"It's for murder, Tommy."

"Okay." He shrugged his shoulders.

Sells agreed to a voluntary search. He was unaware that an armed team in camouflage surrounded the house. Behind the trailer, one of those men streaked across the back, waving a gun. Sells spotted him out the window and poked his head out the back door. For a moment, Pope thought he was going to run for it, and that they would have to shoot him. Sells pulled his head back in, but now he was ticked off. He indicated he might withdraw his permission for the search.

The juvenile investigator, brought along because of the children in the home, blurted out, "We'll just get a search warrant, then." Sells became angry at this retort and withdrew his permission. Then, he relented and gave his approval, but once a search warrant had been threatened, it had to be produced. They all waited for it to be delivered.

THEY found the clothes Sells had worn at the Harris home wadded up in a dirty clothesbasket. Jessica confirmed they were his. Where they lay, they were not visibly stained with blood. Later in the lab, though, the blood would be found and extracted. DNA tests would prove it was the blood of Katy Harris and Krystal Surles. The investigators also took a pair of tennis shoes to see if DPS could match them to a bloody footprint found on the linoleum in the Harris house. They did not match.

Pope and Stamps thought they'd found a possible murder weapon when they uncovered a twelve-inch boning knife. Although it had no obvious signs of blood, it was bagged as evidence.

Sells, however, denied that it was the murder weapon. He explained that he had found two identical knives while cleaning up his father-in-law's butcher shop after a flood. He was referring to the disaster in Del Rio, less than a year and a half earlier, that had killed twenty people, left hundreds homeless and caused monumental property damage throughout the area.

The other knife—the one used in the attack—was no longer in his house. Sells had brought it home with him from the murder. He'd tried to break it, but failed, cutting his own hand in the process. He tried to put it down a sewer pipe, but it was so badly twisted by his attempt to snap it in two that it would not fit. Finally, he threw it into the brush in the empty field by the trailer.

As he left his home, he noticed Jessica being escorted into another patrol car. He demonstrated his first sign of distress. He pleaded for them not to arrest his wife. She'd had nothing to do with this. She knew nothing about it. Officers eased him into the back seat with assurances that they only planned to question Jessica, not charge her.

As soon as Lieutenant Pope pulled away from the house, headed toward the Val Verde County Correctional Center, confession flowed from the back seat. Pope interrupted him, "Do you understand your rights?"

"Yes."

Since, in Texas, a confession must be videotaped or written to be admissible in court, Pope then urged him to wait till they arrived at his office.

After a mile of silence, Sells spoke up. "I guess we have a lot to talk about."

Hoping he would say no more, Pope did not respond.

A moment later, Sells said, "I suppose you want me to tell you about the other one."

Pope stopped breathing. Had he heard right? *"The other one"*? *What other one?* he wondered. His eyes flew up to the rearview mirror and locked in on the eyes reflected there—the cold, cold eyes of a predator.

CHAPTER SIX

SOME kids slip through the cracks. Others, like Tommy Lynn Sells, tumble into crevasses so deep and so cold, no light or warmth can get in. In Lieutenant Larry Pope's words: "Tommy never had anything but the short end of the stick."

He was born a twin on June 28, 1964, in Oakland, California, to Nina Sells, also known as Nina Lovins. His twin sister was Tammy Jean. Publicly, his father was William Sells. When the twins were born, they joined two other siblings, Terry Joe and Timothy Lee. The family was soon enriched with three more boys, twins Jerry Kevin and Jimmy Keith, and then Randy Gene. Tommy Lynn Sells swore that the biological father of all of these children was a man named Joe Lovins, but William Sells legally bore the title of father. He worked a regular job with benefits—most importantly, insurance coverage for a family. When William Sells had serious financial problems, he turned to Lovins, who bailed him out. Tommy Sells claimed, and his mother did not deny, that Lovins, a car salesman and gambler, took advantage of William Sells' debt to force him to claim the children as his own. Joe Lovins is also the man who gave Sells the words that became his motto for two decades of mayhem: "Dead men tell no tales."

Soon after the family moved back to Missouri from Oakland, California, crisis struck. The twins were eighteen months old when Tammy Jean developed an excessively high fever. Nina rushed her to the hospital, arriving at about 6 A.M. The doctor said that the baby had pneumonia, and put her in a plastic tent. Nina sat by her bedside watching as beads of sweat formed and rolled across her little daughter's face and plastered her hair to the top of her head. At 6:30 P.M., Tammy Jean died. Nina did not believe the diagnosis of pneumonia, and insisted on an autopsy. The cause of death was spinal meningitis. As an adult, Tommy commemorated his lost twin with a tattoo on his upper left arm—a tombstone bearing her name.

While Nina and the family attended the funeral, Nina's aunt, Bonnie Walpole, cared for little Tommy. She placed an urgent call. "Nina, Tommy's got an awfully high fever. I'm leaving right now. Meet me at the hospital."

Once again, the same doctor gave the same diagnosis—pneumonia. Nina grabbed Tommy Lynn and said, "You're not going to kill another one of my babies." She ran out of the hospital into a cold and blustering wind. It tore at the blankets wrapped around her son, exposing his body to the elements. The frantic mother barely managed to hang on to the covers but, no matter how she struggled, she could not wrap them around her child. She left the hospital and drove ninety miles to the next one. Halfway there, the feverish child suddenly sat up. Soon he was chattering away and rolling around in the seat as if nothing had happened. When they reached the hospital, a nurse confirmed that Tommy's fever had broken. He remained in the facility for five days, romping in his bed. There was no recurrence of his fever.

SOON after his recovery, Nina decided to rent a home owned by her Aunt Bonnie. When she checked the place out with a sniffling Tommy Lynn in tow, Bonnie offered to keep the toddler until the Sells family settled into their new home.

For two-and-a-half years, the boy lived with Aunt Bonnie. He claimed it was the one bright spot in his childhood. According to his aunt, his favorite pastime was repeatedly riding a tricycle up and down the sidewalk. When he grew up, he wanted to be a fireman.

He received all the attention a toddler could desire from Bonnie's two daughters, 12-year-old Sandy and 8-

year-old Kathie. Every school day, he walked toward the school to meet the girls as they were coming home. The threesome frolicked and giggled through dinner and up to bedtime.

Bonnie and the girls loved the "precious boy" as if he were their own. So much so that Bonnie wanted to make the relationship permanent and legally binding. After all, she said, Nina did not visit her son, she did not inquire about him; in truth, she acted as if she did not know of his existence. But, the moment Bonnie asked to adopt him, everything changed. Nina was furious. She jerked Tommy Lynn out of the only home he could remember and brought him back to hers.

Repeatedly, Bonnie attempted to visit her former charge, but Nina rebuffed her attempts, refusing to allow even one brief hug. Hindsight gave Bonnie Walpole a heavy burden of guilt and regret to carry for not having hired a lawyer and fighting to keep the little boy.

AT the age of seven, Tommy began abusing alcohol with the liquor his maternal grandfather, Pa Brown, kept hidden under the seat of his truck. Around this time, Tommy's attendance at school became sporadic—skipping school started as a challenge and soon became a way of life. "He was the kind of child that, whatever you wanted him to do, he was going to make sure he did not do it. Going to school was one of those things," his mother Nina remembered.

When he was 8, Tommy met a man from the nearby town of Frisbee, Missouri. Frisbee was a small place. "They said the population was ninety-seven, but I think they counted some of the people twice," Sells recalled.

The man began a systematic seduction of the young boy. He took him on trips to Kennett, taught him to shoot pool and spent money on him freely. At first, Tommy's visits to the man's house only lasted a couple of days at a time. Then, they got longer. Every time Nina insisted that Tommy come home, he would have a fit and would not stop begging until she allowed him to return. She let his visits get longer and longer and eventually he was living with the man full time.

Tommy reveled in always having a pocketful of spending money provided by the man; but there was a price tag attached to this newfound bounty. According to Tommy, his mother, his Aunt Bonnie and a psychiatrist who later worked with Sells, the man was a pedophile who sexually abused Tommy and others for years. He never was married, but always had a bevy of boys clamoring around his house.

After the first time the man made Tommy have sex with him, the young boy curled up in a tight ball, alone and lonely. All he'd wanted was to talk to someone—anyone—but no one was there. When questioned by a Missouri Highway Patrol officer in 2000, the man denied these allegations.

Tommy started experimenting with marijuana at the age of ten. Joe Lovins, his presumed biological father, died when Tommy was eleven. The last opportunity to speak to his deceased father brought a rush of emotions.

With tears welling in his eyes, he stood by the coffin. He spoke from his heart. "There's a whole lot in my life that's really messed up, Dad. I'm ready to talk to you now. I wish you didn't have to leave me so soon. I'm really going to miss you."

But his words were cut short. A slap on his rump jerked him from his communion with his deceased father. Ma Brown, his maternal grandmother said, "Stop it. Stop right now and go sit down."

THIRTEEN-YEAR-OLD Tommy was staying at Ma Brown's one night. She was sound asleep when she felt a movement on her bed. Her eyes popped open and there was her naked grandson slipping under the covers with her.

"You'd better get your ass out of this bed and stop this shit."

Tommy did as he was told without delay. He never tried to climb into her bed again.

*   *   *

LATER that year, Tommy walked from Clark's house to his family's trailer to visit his mother and brother. He pulled on the doorknob, but it was locked. When he knocked, he got no response. He pulled himself up on the ledge of the windowsill and peered inside. The usual trail of playthings, discarded clothing and crumpled school papers were nowhere to be seen. "No one was there. Nothing was there besides the trailer. They moved—she met a man from Michigan and they got married. Everyone moved to Michigan. No 'I'll see you later.' No 'Bye.' No nothing," Sells recalled. The young man trudged back up the street alone. None of Sells' family members corroborated this story.

A few days later, he pistol-whipped a woman who'd stirred his anger.

CHAPTER SEVEN

Tommy Lynn Sells left home to live life on his own terms when he was 14 years old. He had vivid memories of the places he'd been, the sights he'd seen: the magnificence of the Grand Canyon, the splendor of Niagara Falls, the shouting strips of light in Las Vegas.

But his memory of his first murder was very vague. He was not even sure which one was first and what state he was in at the time. He does remember that in one of his first homicides, he killed a man "in self-preservation" in Mississippi.

On July 5, 1979, just outside of the small town of Port Gibson, Mississippi, Kathleen Cade called her husband at his John Deere dealership and arranged to rendezvous at 5:30 at a T-ball game that their 5-year-old son Richard was playing that night. She then loaded him and John, Jr., their 10-year-old son, in the car and left the house.

Soon after midnight, Richard was asleep in his own bed, John and John, Jr., had drifted off watching TV in the master bedroom and Kathleen stirred awake on the easy chair in the living room. She padded down the hall to her room and wriggled under the sheets, putting John, Jr., between his two parents.

At some point that night, an acne-scarred young man got a stool from the patio and placed it beneath a window on the front of the house. He removed the screen, climbed in the open window and lowered himself to the floor without a sound. He was carrying a .32-caliber Saturday night special.

He scurried into hiding to listen and make sure everyone was deep in sleep. Sometime later, he emerged and went into the kitchen. He pulled a jug of milk out of the refrigerator. He popped the cap and dropped it on the kitchen counter. He swigged from the container as he explored the house. He set the milk down on the floor in the family den, a room in the pathway from the kitchen to the bedrooms. When deputies arrived after 3 A.M., the milk was still cold.

Kathleen heard some rustling and scuffling sounds, but she could not pull herself up out of her deep sleep. Then, she was aware of noises that sounded like popcorn popping in the kitchen or the very distant crack of thunder. Still, she could not reach the surface to wakefulness. But when she heard her husband shout, "What's going on here?" she broke through the fog. Her eyes opened. The first sight she saw was the digital alarm clock on her nightstand. The time was 3:01. She turned to her husband. He turned on the light. "I'm bleeding," he said as he looked down at his hands.

He went into the bathroom. His terrified wife and son were fast on his heels. He bent over the sink to rinse off his hands. He toppled back onto the floor, dead. Kathleen and John, Jr., could only stare in disbelief.

Investigators were baffled. There were no fingerprints, and nothing was missing from the home. The first natural suspect, his wife Kathleen, was given a polygraph test and was cleared of any complicity in the crime. They could find no reasonable explanation for why anyone would want to kill this 39-year-old chairman of the church board, who didn't seem to have an enemy in the world.

IN 1980 in Los Angeles, near a Chinese restaurant, Tommy Lynn Sells killed a man with an ice pick. In Oakland, he tangled in a gang-related fight. Wounded himself, Sells didn't stick around to be sure the other man was dead. When asked later by Lieutenant Larry Pope if he'd killed the man, Tommy said, "I ought to, I stabbed him a bunch of times." Sells was seriously injured. The ice-pick stab he took in the back "missed his spine by a pencil lead."

In the hospital after the skirmish, the nurse came in, lifted the sheet and prepared to insert a urinary catheter. Tommy was outraged. She insisted it was necessary because of bleeding in his kidneys. He still refused. She assumed he objected to a woman performing the procedure, so she sent in a male doctor. He lifted the sheet and he, too, was sworn out of the room. Sells would not have his dignity assaulted by the insertion of a catheter—not even to save his life. He left the hospital against medical advice and hitchhiked to St. Louis where his mother lived once again after leaving her husband in Michigan. It took him forty-nine hours to reach her home. She nursed him back to health.

In the early eighties, Sells spent time in the Little Rock area in Arkansas. He had a brief stint in the now-defunct youth home behind McClellan High School. Then he and a girlfriend took up residence in Southeast Little Rock in an apartment at 6 Portsmouth Drive. She was one of a long string of conquests. His promiscuity was so rampant, his mother took to calling him her "little whore." "He has the gift of gab. He can make any woman believe him. He had more women than Carter had liver pills," she said.

In May of 1981, Nina Sells and the rest of her boys were living in Arkansas, too. She was tired all the time, working two jobs to support her family since her husband died. She was taking a shower one morning before going to work when she heard the bathroom door creak open. Then the shower curtain pulled back and her son, Tommy, joined her in the stall. Nina yelled at him to get out. She kicked his shins. She pummeled his shoulders with her fists. At that moment, she wanted to kill her son and have him out of her life for good. Tommy jumped out of the shower, put on his clothes and fled the house.

He was admitted as an outpatient to the Community Mental Health Clinic in Jonesboro, Arkansas, for the attempted sexual assault of his mother. He was prompt for his first appointment, but obviously confused.

"I don't know who I am," he admitted. His tortured hazel eyes looked briefly at the counselor, then flashed away, concentrating on the floor.

"Do you know why you attacked your mother, Tommy?"

He shook his head. "I feel like a fool for trying to attack Mom. I don't understand why I did it. I don't understand anything anymore."

"Were you angry?"

"Yes." His eyes flared with brilliance as he remembered the heat of his emotion.

"Why, Tommy? What did your mother do?"

"She tries to run my life. I'm going to run my own life, and I don't care who I have to hurt to do it."

The clinician observed his facial expressions, general body movements and the amplitude and quality of his speaking voice, and knew with a certainty that Tommy was an angry, volatile young man.

In testing, a more complete picture of the troubled adolescent was revealed. He felt unwanted and unloved. He thought he was the cause of all the problems in the home. He was sad, in pain and unhappy about his current situation. He wanted to strike out and hurt someone else to relieve his own feelings of pain.

His diagnosis found him to be engaged in alcohol and cannabis abuse. It also said he suffered from conduct disorder, under-socialization and aggression. It was recommended that he attend regular therapy sessions to explore his feelings and anger and "[. . .] to find alternative methods of ventilation of his emotions in a safe, non-threatening environment and non-damaging manner." Sells attended five therapy sessions. On June 18, he called in and cancelled his sixth appointment. He never returned to the clinic again.

On March 27, 1982, Tommy Lynn Sells was arrested in Little Rock for public intoxication after a disturbance at an apartment complex on Geyer Springs Road. At the time, he was working at the Kinney Shoe Store on that same street.

He fathered a boy in Arkansas in 1982, with a woman named Cindy Hanna. Cindy was his first love, but the odds were stacked against the couple. Cindy's father strongly disapproved of Sells. The fact that he had robbed the church the Hannas attended did not endear him to the family.

SELLS later confessed to two murders during his time in this area. One has been verified, but with a slightly different outcome.

He crept up to the home in a wooded area just south of the Pulaski–Saline County Line at 14715 Chicot Road. He did not plan to harm anyone. He just wanted to break in and steal what he could. Unfortunately for Hal Akins, he was at home when Sells came calling. When caught in the act, Sells ran and Hal followed. Without warning, Tommy turned and fired a shot. Hal dropped to the ground, held his breath and pretended to be dead. Tommy believed that he had killed him. But Tommy was wrong. And Hal was lucky.

TOMMY and an accomplice kidnapped a woman seven miles southwest of Little Rock at a fast-food restaurant. They took her down a dirt road to a bluff overlooking a 100-foot-deep lake. The trilling songs of birds and the rustle of leaves caressed by a breeze provided a harmonic backdrop to the screams of a tormented young woman. When they were through with her, the scent of fear, seminal fluid and blood overwhelmed the fresh fragrance of the forest. One grabbed the arms, the other picked up the legs of the dead victim. They gave her body a swing and heaved her into one of the water-filled rock quarries that folks in southern Pulaski County call "blue holes."

SELLS was fairly stationary in 1983, living in the 3300 block of Edmundson in Breckenridge Hills near St. Louis, Missouri. He managed to accumulate three traffic tickets in the area that year, in June, July and December.

Thomas and Colleen Gill and their two children were residents of the West End neighborhood of St. Louis at that same time. They owned and operated Colette & Thomas on Hair, Ltd., a beauty salon in Des Peres. They bought their large home at 23 Washington Terrace in need of repair and renovation in January 1983.

On July 31, a man matching Sells' description was seen fleeing the Gill family home, just as Thomas Gill was pulling up to the house. When Gill walked inside, the bloody, bludgeoned bodies of his wife and his 4-year-old daughter, Tiffany, greeted him chillingly. He raced upstairs to his 1-year-old son, Sean. The boy was sleeping soundly, unaware of the insanity that had erupted downstairs.

The neighborhood had been plagued by burglaries, but Colleen still wore a generous diamond ring on her hand. Suspicions shifted to Thomas Gill because he had purchased a $600,000 life insurance policy on his wife only three weeks before. But suspicion never amounted to indictable proof—and Gill was never arrested.

ON May 8, 1984, Sells was under arrest by the Scott County Sheriff's Department in Benton, Missouri. He was charged with stealing a Ford Mustang and released in custody to Dunklin County. There he pleaded guilty to the felony and was sentenced to two years in the state penitentiary system by a judge who was the father of one of Sells' grade school friends. While serving his sentence, Sells' daughter was born to Nicole Snow.

He entered the Missouri State Penitentiary, now known as the Jefferson City Correctional Center, on September 18, 1984. At the time, it was known as "The Walls." Convicts simply called it "God's bloodiest forty acres on earth." Minor infractions for creating a disturbance bounced him to Algoa Correctional Center, then to Boonville and then back to Algoa. From there, he was paroled on February 18, 1985.

• • •

IN July, he stole another car, drove it to Rolla, Missouri, and abandoned it at a doughnut shop. On the 19th, he checked into the New Horizons Rehabilitation Center in Vichy, Missouri, fifteen miles to the north. Three days later, his mother informed law enforcement of his location, and an officer from Clayton, Missouri, interviewed him by telephone about the car theft. Soon another phone call came, this one from his parole officer. Concerned that he'd be picked up on a parole violation, Sells fled the rehab center.

Days later a woman and her 5-year-old boy lay dead because Tommy Lynn Sells got angry.

CHAPTER EIGHT

IN the southwestern corner of Missouri lies the city of Springfield. It bills itself as "The Gateway to the Ozarks." Traveling south, the terrain gets hillier, the countryside less tame.

The Ozarks are an old range of mountains. The ragged peaks that once heaved up from the earth in a cataclysmic event have eroded with the passage of time. Now, the mountains are rolling pillows accented by dramatic valleys.

The White River raced through the Ozarks in Taney County where dams built between 1911 and 1958 created three lakes heralded for their bass fishing, and as a source for hydroelectric power. The county bordering the State of Arkansas had a population of less than 10,000 in the mid-eighties. It wasn't a very diverse group—98 percent of the populace was white.

In the summertime, the sides of back roads are littered with wildflowers—the brilliant red of Indian paintbrush, the pulsating pink of dianthus, the golden glow of goat's beard. The Mark Twain National Forest covers a large portion of the wild and beautiful county.

In the shadow of this forest, nestled at the mouth of Swan Creek, is the county seat of Forsyth. It is a town that clings fast to its past. It's a place where you can still experience a flashback to the fifties in an old-fashioned café with red-and-white oilskin tablecloths and a worn linoleum floor.

The slow, peaceful environs of Forsyth and the breathtaking beauty of its surroundings were permanently scarred when the carnival came to town.

ON Friday, July 26, 1985, Rory "Willie" Cordt was excited about turning five in eight days. He was a cute boy with a bowl-shaped haircut and a smile that seemed two sizes too big for his little face. He was looking forward to starting kindergarten in the fall. At the moment, though, he was just about beside himself because he was going to the carnival at the Taney County Fair with his mother, Ena Cordt, a pretty and petite woman with brown hair and dark eyes. Willie thrilled at the lights, the rides, the games he could only dream of winning. And dream he did, like any other little boy: visions of being older and bigger; hopes of one day winning that enormous teddy bear and giving it to his mommy with pride.

Awestruck, he clutched his mother's hand, reveling in the dirt and sawdust underfoot, the smell of cotton candy and popcorn in the air and the roar of the crowd and the machinery. He immersed himself in a wild, wonderful world of 4-year-old fantasy. Reality, though, was waiting at that carnival for Willie and Ena: waiting in the shape of a man—a man named Tommy Lynn Sells.

Life gets a little lonely for a divorced mother in a small town. After years as a maintenance worker at Skaggs Hospital in Branson, she now toiled away at a car wash in Forsyth during the day and cared for her son at night. Maybe she was looking for a little excitement. Maybe she just took pity on a young man and invited him over for a home-cooked meal. Or maybe she thought she'd seen the last of him after some harmless flirtation on the carnival grounds and had no idea he was coming to visit that night. Ena can no longer let us know.

The seductive words he whispered to her in the shadow of the Ferris wheel that night led her to the worst decision in her twenty-eight years of life. Like a leaf in a whirlpool, she was drawn into his world of uncontrollable violence.

•   •   •

THE yard of the split-level home on Willow Lane was littered with balls, toys and other signs of a child. Inside, the
rooms were clean but slightly disheveled. It was late when
Tommy arrived, and little Willie was in bed.

According to Tommy it was a pleasant visit, up to a
point. He excused himself to use the bathroom.

While he was out of the room, Ena looked through
Tommy's knapsack. Perhaps she was just curious and
wanted to know a bit more about the stranger in her home.
Had he given her his real name? Was he really from Missouri? Show me.

Unfortunately, she took too long in her inspection.
When Tommy emerged from the bathroom, he caught her
pink negligee–clad body bent over his bag. Without a moment's doubt, he concluded that she was after his stash of
cocaine. Convinced she was trying to steal his drugs, he
flew into a rage. *No one steals from Tommy Lynn Sells. No
one treats him like a punk.*

He roared down the hallway, spotted little Willie's
baseball bat along the way and snatched it up without slow-
ing his pace in his race toward Ena. She froze in the icy
glare of his cold eyes. He lifted the bat high in the air and
slammed it down with fury. Viciously he beat her on the
head, on her upraised arms, on her bowed back. She
screamed. She begged for help. She prayed for her neighbors to hear. And then her horror intensified, multiplied.
Willie stood framed in the doorway, frightened and powerless, crying and pleading for it all to stop. But it was too
late for Ena. She could not comfort her son. She was not
able to put up much of a struggle. She could not escape.
The blows were too hard, too fast, too final. Her skull was
fractured. And now Sells brandished a knife from her
kitchen. One quick slice to her throat and Ena was gone.
Her body slumped by the end table.

Sells noticed Willie, too. He stepped over the battered,
lifeless body of Ena. And in two strides, his hand grasped

the scrawny little arm of the 4-year-old boy and dragged him into the living room. All the while, he beat Willie on the head with the boy's own baseball bat, then slit his throat with his mother's knife and dropped the still body to the floor by the couch. It did not matter that Willie was only 4. All that mattered was that he was a witness. And Joe Lovins had warned Tommy that a witness should never be left alive.

When his rage was spent, Sells calmly removed all identifying traces of his presence from the home, wiping away fingerprints and gathering his belongings. Carrying Willie's bat, he forced his way out of the bloody house through a seldom-used door and fled anonymously into the night. Carnival workers often disappeared on a whim. His absence raised no suspicions.

ENA and Willie's bodies lay cold and unnoticed for three days. At seven in the evening on July 30, 1985, Ena's parents, Bob and Jill McIntosh, made the gruesome discovery. Her red car was parked out front, but not a sound came from inside the house when they knocked on the door. They pushed it open and the smell of rotting flesh assaulted their nostrils. Then their eyes consumed the blood spattered on the walls and puddled on the floor. In the midst of all this carnage, the battered and bloated bodies of their daughter and grandson lay crumpled on the floor.

On the day Willie should have been celebrating his fifth birthday, he was instead buried in the ground beside his mother at Snapps cemetery in rural Taney County. To the relief of the family, Ena's other child, 8-year-old Peggy, was still alive. She had spent that part of her summer vacation visiting her father.

LAW enforcement was left with no motive, no firm suspects, and no solution to a double homicide in a small town. And Tommy Lynn Sells was left on the loose.

CHAPTER NINE

IT was soon obvious that Sells' visit to the rehabilitation center had not been a success. On September 4, 1985, Sells, drunk and drugged, drove down the road with two underage girls. He lost control of his vehicle, causing it to flip and roll three times. All three occupants walked away from the scene with only minor injuries. Because of this incident, Sells was arrested in Missouri for driving while intoxicated and for charges related to the minor girls. Thirty days later, the court dropped the charges related to his driving companions for time served.

On October 15, his parole revoked, he returned to Missouri State Penitentiary. On the 29th of October, he transferred back to Boonville Correctional Center. His violations behind bars were infrequent and minor—creating a disturbance and self-mutilation. He was released with his sentence served in full on May 16, 1986.

CHAPTER TEN

WHEN Crystal Harris was a teenager in Kansas, she made a number of foolish decisions. Early in 1985, she got pregnant and married the father of the child she was carrying. In November, at the age of 17, she became the mother of Justin. He was blind from birth. Ten months later, her daughter, Kaylene, was born. Lori came next, just sixteen months later.

One month after Lori's debut into the world, the 20-year-old Crystal filed for divorce. She packed up her meager belongings and removed her brood from the explosive atmosphere of an abusive home.

She bought a place of her own and settled into a lively home that bounced with the kinetic presence of three toddlers. In 1990, she met a neighbor, Terry Harris. Their relationship started as a friendship, but soon spilled over into romance. Gun-shy from her first encounter with matrimony, Crystal was reluctant to even discuss walking down the aisle until she was certain she was not making another mistake. Instead, she invited Terry and Shawn, his first-grade son, to move in with her nest of rug rats. This decision horrified her parents but, since it didn't cause a permanent family rift, it suited Crystal well.

The blended family built a foundation of trust and love in Kansas for the next five years. When Katy went off to kindergarten, she became aware that she was different from the other children in her class. They all had a mommy and a daddy. She had a mommy and a Terry. She crawled into his lap one evening and asked, "Would you be my Daddy?"

"Yes," Terry said, smothering her with an emotional hug.

Crystal raised an eyebrow at his response. She and Terry had not yet discussed marriage.

AFTER leaving prison, Sells worked for Atlas Towing in St. Louis for a short time. He drove a one-ton tow truck and a big tow rig, hauling vehicles and making emergency roadside repairs. While employed in this capacity, he met and married a woman named Sandy who has since died of breast cancer.

One night, about five minutes from the Arch just off Broadway in downtown St. Louis, he was repairing the vehicle of a stranded motorist. Without provocation, he claimed, the man kicked him. Sells pulled his gun, shot the man and left him for dead. Before he could leave the area, he was arrested in Pagedale Township just outside of St. Louis for stealing a light bar from one of the tow trucks. The charges were dropped and Sells resumed his nomadic existence, criss-crossing the country.

SELLS meandered south until he reached Aransas Pass, Texas, a seedy little fishing town separated from the Gulf of Mexico by the outlying Mustang Island. There, he got a job with Gulf Team Shrimp. Their shrimping boats went out to sea for thirty days at a stretch. On one of these trips, he overdosed on heroin. He turned blue and passed out before he could push all of the heroin. He was discovered with the needle still stuck in his arm. When James, the rig man, found him, his breathing was labored. Since the boat was two-and-a-half days from the dock—and proper medical care—his survival was questionable. Bobby, the captain, called the Coast Guard. Before they arrived, Sells regained consciousness. He was still alive when the boat reached shore.

After that harrowing experience, he did not go back to sea. Instead, he floated across the nation, going wherever impulse led him. There were violent encounters along this journey. He may have killed 19-year-old Michelle Xavier and 20-year-old Jennifer Duey in Fremont, California, in 1986. Their bodies were discovered off Mill Creek Road. One was shot in the head, the other's throat was sliced wide open.

In late April 1987, Sells hopped a freight train and rode it as far north as he could go. He disembarked in Lockport, New York, near Niagara Falls. In that town, on May 1, Susan Korcz was in a local bar fighting with her boyfriend, Michael Mandell. She stomped out in disgust, heading in a direction that would not have taken her home. She was never seen again. She was listed as a missing person.

Leads were followed and suspects questioned with no results. Susan did not show up or call the hair salon where she worked as a beautician. There was no activity on her credit cards or in her bank account. She did not contact her family. Within weeks, Susan Korcz was presumed dead. Police conducted canal and waterway searches but did not find her body.

In the center of Lockport is the Niagara escarpment. Some of the hillsides take an abrupt fifty- to sixty-foot drop. Near the escarpment, a canal with a series of locks gives the town its name. More than seven years after Susan's disappearance, a worker from a plant was sent up on the hill to clear off the debris. He saw what he initially thought was a piece of trash, but when he picked it up, he realized it was a human skull. Susan Korcz's body had finally been found, 800 feet from the canal, near a railroad trestle. She had been buried in a shallow grave covered with debris. Due to the advanced state of decomposition, the cause of death was unknown.

On May 3, 1987, two days after Susan's disappearance, and two states away, Sells awoke with blood all over his clothes.

CHAPTER ELEVEN

SELLS wandered aimlessly toward the Southwest until he came to a stop in Humboldt County, Nevada. It is a desolate area where the largest employers are in the mining industry. Since the early 1800s, they've pulled silver, copper, molybdenum, tungsten, iron, bauxite, clay and mercury out of the ground. It's a countryside spotted with hot springs and abandoned mines. To the south of the county, in the shadow of Bloody Run Peak, is the small town of Winnemucca, population nearly 13,000 in 1987.

Arriving in that town, Sells worked for the Raymond Lavoie Roofing company. But his expenses were bigger than his paycheck. He passed a bad check on October 28. Then on the 30th, he stole a bank bag and a handgun from his employer's truck and used Raymond Lavoie's credit card to rent a hotel room for a woman.

STEFANIE Stroh, a 20-year-old student at Reed College in Oregon and long-time resident of San Francisco, had just returned from her ten-month trip to Europe and Asia. When she flew into New York, she decided to fulfill her lifelong dream of hitchhiking across the United States with a friend. They traveled together as far as Salt Lake City. She called home nearly every day and her mother mentally plotted her cross-country progress. She was not too worried—Stefanie never told her she was hitchhiking.

On October 15, at Four Way Truck Stop in Wells, Nevada, Stefanie Stroh went to the pay phone and called her parents collect. After a breathless description of the sights she had seen since the last call, she told them where she was and assured them she would be home in a couple of days.

The next day, she was in Winnemucca at the Motel 6. No rooms were available and she asked about the possibility of accommodations in Reno, planning to continue her journey down Route 80.

As Tommy Lynn Sells told the Texas Rangers, he zeroed in on the young woman on the side of the road. She looked better and better the closer he got to her. The 5'5" large-breasted woman with sun-bleached dark brown hair was dressed in hippie-style clothing, and carrying an orange sleeping bag roll and a gray backpack with two small drums attached. She stuck out her thumb as Sells approached, presenting him with an opportunity he could not resist. Coming to a stop, he pushed the passenger door open. Stefanie ran over to the pick-up truck and paused at the door.

"Where are you headed?" she asked.

"Where you want to go?" he answered.

"Reno."

"Hop in. I'm heading that way."

Stefanie swiveled into the passenger seat, filled with relief. Near Lovelock, Sells turned off the highway with an invitation instead of an explanation. "I've got some acid. You want to drop some with me?"

Since she had already taken major risks hitchhiking across the country, drug experimentation in the desert no longer seemed extreme. While waiting for the effects of the drug to transport her to another place, she regaled Sells with tales of Paris. Then, high on LSD in the surreal environment of the desert, her life crystallized and shattered into pieces as Sells choked her to death.

In the stolen truck Sells drove that day, the vehicle's owner had a convenient washtub and a bag of quick-mix concrete. Sells placed Stefanie's feet into the tub, mixed up and poured in the concrete and left her hanging off the tailgate of the pick-up overnight while the concrete hardened.

In the morning, he dragged her weighted body, her gray backpack and other belongings over to a thirty-foot-wide hot spring. It was not one of the tame bodies of water that attracted droves of people to soak in comforting warmth. Anyone sticking their toes in this spring would deeply regret their recklessness. He dropped her in feet-first, watched her sink into the bubbling water and drove out of the desert.

THREE days later, when their daughter had not arrived home and had not called, Stefanie's mother and stepfather, Joni and Grant Settlemeir, called the Winnemucca Police Department and filed a missing persons report. When authorities ascertained that Stefanie had been hitch-hiking across the country, it was easy to jump to the conclusion that she had been abducted across state lines. Because of this assumption, the FBI was on the case by mid-November.

In no time, Marvin Stroh, Stefanie's father, was on the scene with nine friends and family members. They traveled from the airport straight to the Chrysler dealership. Stroh purchased eight Jeeps outright and set out to find his daughter. Because the last call received from Stefanie came from Wells in Elko County, the search began there. Then they got word about Stefanie's presence in Winnemucca and turned their attention to Humboldt County.

Ranger Coy Smith, long familiar with the desolation of West Texas, was amazed by the emptiness he found in this part of Nevada. "It is the end of the world out there," the Ranger said. "You can drive for days and there ain't nothing."

And drive for days they did—into the desert and down Route 80 to Reno. All along the way, they plastered up posters and asked questions. Then they focused on Reno itself, stopping at moderate- and low-priced hotels to see if Stefanie had ever made it that far down Route 80. Without success, they returned to the dealership, sold back the Jeeps and flew back to the West Coast.

The search fliers were posted everywhere in Winne-mucca and Reno as well as up and down the interstate for miles. Authorities conducted interviews at all the truck stops in Humboldt and surrounding counties. Motel 6, where she had stopped looking for a room, provided names and addresses of everyone staying there on October 16, in hopes that someone had seen her after she left the front desk. They asked questions at any other place someone might stop when traveling through the area. Joni Settlemeir made television appearances pleading for information about Stefanie. Any resident of Nevada would have been hard-pressed not to be aware of her disappearance.

But the task of law enforcement was onerous. Route 80 is the most well-traveled truck route in the country with 32,000 to 36,000 vehicles passing through every twenty-four hours. The isolation in the surrounding countryside complicated their search even more. "You could go one quarter of a mile off the freeway and never see another person walking or a cowboy on horseback," said former Humboldt County Sheriff James Bagwell. "You could hide a body out there and nobody would find it—ever."

The city of San Francisco offered a $10,000 reward for information leading to Stefanie, or to the person or persons responsible for her disappearance.

The Stroh family hired a psychic to aid in their search. They were told that they could find Stefanie's body in the bottom of a well or a mine near an eastern Nevada town with four syllables in its name. Both Winnemucca and Battle Mountain fit that description. There would be a white building, a ravine and strip mining nearby. And finally, the psychic said, "I see her feet in concrete."

Authorities scouted the area. They found an old road-house that matched the psychic's profile. The abandoned dry well there could have been a substitute for a ravine. Chief Mike Curti called in the city fire rescue truck with its powerful lights. He peered with binoculars down the shaft, but the light did not penetrate the depths.

The police chief called the sheriff's department and

they brought their video camera out to the old well. They lowered it down and got back tape of the scene below. Although the images were sharp enough to identify an old television antenna and other debris, there was no sign of Stefanie Stroh.

The family requested an aerial search of the area in hopes of finding elusive clues. A pilot on his way to California to pick up a prisoner was willing to do the job. Low and slow, with camera rolling, he scanned the area between Winnemucca and Lovelock on the chance the girl had been slain and thrown off the highway.

In late November, a Winnemucca resident reported an incident she'd observed around the time Stefanie disappeared. She said she was traveling along the frontage road when she saw a girl matching Stefanie's description in a scuffle with a truck driver at the side of the highway. She stopped and asked if she should call the sheriff, but the girl did not respond. The man jumped into his rig and the woman walked westward on the highway.

In a few days, another woman stepped forward offering a different version of events. She claimed the man was walking along the highway and a woman drove up in a rig, got out of the truck and a scuffle ensued. This woman did get the name of the truck company, making it possible to track the identity of the driver. Soon, the FBI got a name from the Arkansas-based trucking firm. But the man was no longer employed by that business and his location was unknown.

From diner to lunch counter, Winnemucca buzzed about nothing else as they downed their cups of coffee. In time, no news was reported and interest waned in the community—no one there actually knew the girl. On several occasions, over the years, someone stumbled across unidentified human remains out in the desert. The buzz would pick up again and each time, the family and friends of Stefanie Stroh held their collective breaths. But Stefanie was never found. If she had been, the answers would be clear.

As it now stands, some law enforcement officials believe Sells' version of events. Others do not.

NEITHER his friends nor his employer knew of any plans to leave Winnemucca, but on November 3, Sells was heading out of town, trolling again. In a matter of days, he made it to Illinois and committed the most gruesome murders of his life.

CHAPTER TWELVE

NOTHING earth-shattering ever happened in the sleepy town of Ina in southern Illinois. The small village was home to a gas station, a bank, a store, a post office, a firehouse and just enough houses and trailers for its 475 residents. On the night of November 17, 1987, a deadly fear and uncertainty was born in the hearts of the citizens of Ina that will haunt them all for the rest of their lives.

Of the four people present in the house on the southern edge of town that night, only Tommy Lynn Sells remains alive. And he has told three different stories about his fatal encounter with the family. In one version, Keith Dardeen picked him up while he was hitchhiking and brought him home. In another, he met Keith at the pool hall and was invited to his house. In the third, he knocked on the front door and forced his way inside. In the first two versions, he claims the two of them were driving down the road later in the evening, when Keith made a homosexual advance. That threw Sells into a blind rage.

By most accounts, Keith was not the type of man to pick up hitchhikers or to bring a stranger home to his family. He was very protective of his house, his wife and his son. He was not likely to allow entry to a stranger at the door. There is also no evidence pointing to any homosexual activity or fantasy in any corner of Keith's life. The conclusions of authorities and others close to the case were blended with portions of Sells' recollections to reconstruct the most likely sequence of events that night.

Riding the rails through Illinois, Tommy Lynn Sells jumped off the train in Ina near Route 57, a major highway running north to south through the state. To the north, it passes by Champaign-Urbana and Kankakee, and then into Chicago. Where he disembarked, the highway passes south through a series of small whistle-stop towns until it ends near the Kentucky state line.

Like any predator, his eyes constantly sought signs of vulnerability, open doors to opportunity. The modest trailer beckoned to him. It had a "for sale" sign propped in the window—a perfect prop for Sells. The Dardeens rented the property from Lloyd and Joann Settle, who farmed the land near the house site. But, though the Dardeens owned the trailer, it was beginning to feel too small for their now-growing family. Their new baby was due early in the new year.

Sells sat in the darkness overlooking the home, waiting, watching and drinking one beer after another. When he determined the time was ripe, he approached the home with caution, his hand wrapped tightly around the gun he had stolen in Nevada, which was now securely concealed in his pocket. He knocked on the door as he shivered on the doorstep. When Keith opened it, he asked the stranger what he wanted. Sells said he was interested in buying the mobile home.

Keith had not heard a car pull up. Looking over the stranger's shoulder, he would have seen that only his own vehicles were parked in the drive. Aware of his responsibility to his pregnant wife, Elaine, and his three-year-old son, Peter, Keith suppressed his desire for a sale. He refused to let Sells come in and look at the trailer. As he closed the door, Sells threw his body into the open gap, pulled his gun and pointed it at Keith's head.

Sells shouted threats and obscenities and Keith backed up, his hands raised above his head. A few yards away, Elaine clutched little Peter to her side, frozen in fear. At a shout from Keith, she turned to flee to the bedroom with her son. Sells was too quick. He grabbed Peter and held the gun to his head.

"Shut up. Everything's gonna be fine so long as you

all do what I say," Sells reassured them. Motioning to Keith he said, "You got any rope?"

"I don't think so," Keith stammered.

Sells jerked the gun against little Peter's head, causing the boy to emit a shrieking sob. He gave him a shake. "Shut up." Then he turned to Keith and ordered, "Find something to tie them up."

After fumbling through kitchen drawers, Keith produced a roll of duct tape. Without moving the gun from the little boy's head, Sells bound Peter's feet, hands and mouth with the tape. Dragging the constrained boy with him, he ordered Elaine to the floor, where he repeated the binding process with her. This would be Keith and Elaine's last chance to see one another—to exchange eye contact, to see the tears in one another's eyes. Sells told Elaine that if she moved, her husband was dead.

Then, he turned to Keith and threatened to kill his wife and child if he did not obey, and forced him out of the home at gunpoint. With a gun to his head, Keith drove his car a mile away to an empty field full of left-over stubble on the campus of Rend Lake College. When the car stopped, Keith knew he had to wrest the gun away. If he did not, he would be dead. If he died, there would be no one to protect his beloved Elaine and Peter. He made his first move. Tommy countered with a gunshot into his cheek. Keith slumped back.

Sells dragged his limp body from the car and threw him on the ground. Keith made weak protests and feeble gestures of struggle. Sells unzipped Keith's pants, pulled out the man's penis and cut it from his body. He waved it in his face and said, "I'm taking this to your wife."

Sells then shot the dying man twice—in the side of his face and in the side of his head.

SOAKED in the bloodlust of the moment, Sells jumped into Keith's car and drove back to the trailer. When the door flew open, Elaine's eyes registered hope. When she saw who walked through the door, hope turned to horror.

Sells unbound her feet in order to rape her. Using scissors, he cut off her clothing. When she struggled, he threatened to kill her son if she did not cooperate. Instantly, she became still and accepted the assault with barely a whimper behind the duct tape that sealed her mouth shut.

While she lay on the floor, used and helpless, Sells roamed through the trailer. Her mind raced—wondering what had happened to Keith and seeking a means of escape, a way to get help. Peter was crying uncontrollably. His sobs stuck to the back of the tape. She wanted to speak words of comfort to him, to touch him, to hold him. All she could do was send a message of love from her eyes to his.

Sells raised little Peter's baseball bat high in the air and slammed it into the head of the three-year-old lying small and bound at his feet. Elaine struggled to her feet and rushed at her tormentor just as he raised the bat again. This time, he only grazed Peter's head.

He shoved Elaine backwards. Hands bound, she lost her balance and fell to the floor. He raised the bat over Peter and hit him again and again until he was certain the child was dead. Then, he turned back to Elaine. He hit her once, then raised the bat, ready to hit her again. He paused. Something unusual was happening. Elaine had gone into premature labor. Before his eyes, a three-pound, thirteen-ounce baby girl was being born. Coldly he watched until the infant had emerged.

He looked at Elaine. He saw the desperate pleading in her eyes. He smiled. A sharp intake of hope caught in her throat. From somewhere he picked up a knife. He wielded it now, slicing into her breasts. Then, he turned to the baby, who was still attached to her mother through the umbilical cord. He raised his bat high and beat her until she was dead.

Now, all Elaine wanted was to die. Tommy Lynn Sells obliged her. He beat her in the head, fracturing her skull. As the last breath of life fled her body and dissipated into the night, he sexually assaulted her with the bat, leaving it lodged deep inside her.

• • •

THE night was over for the Dardeens. But not for their killer. He had work to do. He had evidence to eliminate. He carried the bodies of Elaine, Peter and Casey into the master bedroom and laid them carefully on the bed. He removed all but the most microscopic traces of duct tape from their cooling bodies. He stuffed all the pieces into his pockets.

He cleaned up after himself, going room to room. On the coat rack, a Toucan Sam painter's cap hung, bearing silent witness to his efforts. He wiped surfaces for finger-prints, cleaned up puddles of blood, sought any place that identifying traces could hide, and sanitized them. It was a slow, meticulous process. It spoke of a man who had killed before. It warned of a man who would kill again.

WHEN he was satisfied that the job was complete, he climbed back into Keith's blood-spattered, red 1981 Plymouth and headed south on Highway 57.

CHAPTER THIRTEEN

On Wednesday, when Keith Dardeen did not show up for work at the treatment plant for Rend Lake Water Conservancy District, his supervisor called his home. When he got no answer there all day, he was concerned. Keith was a responsible and dependable employee. That evening, he called Keith's father. Don Dardeen was just as puzzled as he was. Although Don was divorced from Keith's mother, Joeann Dardeen, he lived near her in the neighboring town of Mount Carmel.

He went over to her home where his daughter, Anita Knapp, and her two sons, 7-year-old Eddie and 4-year-old Robbie, had come over for pizza. Joeann knew an unexplained absence was out of character for her son. She called the sheriff's office and Don drove to Ina to meet them with the house key.

As the door swung open, what they found sent waves of fear crashing on the village of Ina. But there was only one adult body laid out on the bed. Not two. The missing person was Keith Dardeen, and he instantly became a suspect. Many minds in the community came to the same conclusion. It was only natural. Statistically, it was logical. And for the residents of Jefferson County, it dredged up the memory of a not-too-distant event.

Just four-and-a-half years earlier, and only ten miles up Route 57, in the town of Mount Vernon, another family had been visited by unspeakable tragedy: 19-year-old Thomas Odle had murdered his parents and his three siblings. He quietly ambushed them one by one as they arrived home from work or school. Many wondered and others assumed that one more man had erupted in a rage that sent his family to the grave.

WHEN the doorbell rang at Joeann's house, Eddie and Robbie ran to answer it. When they did, they looked into the muzzles of guns held by four police officers.

Upon hearing the news of the discovery at her son's home, Joeann paced the room. "Oh, God! Oh, God! Where's Keith?"

Officers escorted Joeann into her bedroom and questioned her about Keith's whereabouts. They asked her about the baby in the house. She insisted there was no baby, unaware of the brutal birth of her only granddaughter.

No matter how much law enforcement pushed and accused, Keith's family and friends were adamant. They knew it was impossible for Keith to commit such a callous and violent act. They spurred the sheriff's department to find the man they hoped was still alive, but now feared was dead. Late the next night, hunters discovered Keith's brutalized body, abandoned and discarded in a lonely wheat field just over the Franklin County Line. Then, his car was found. It was as if the killer was thumbing his nose at the authorities and the community. The bloodstained Plymouth was parked with impudence near the police station in Benton, eleven miles away.

Overnight, shotguns popped up in pick-up truck racks all over the county. It was basketball season, and post-game normally meant a gaggle of loud teenagers gathered outside the high school making plans, waiting for rides and just horsing around. Now all that changed. When the game ended, all of the kids huddled inside the building. They did not exit until parents came in and escorted them to their cars.

Rumors raced rampant throughout the area. There was a serial killer stalking southern Illinois. It must have been satanic ritual because of what was done to the mother and

the baby. It had to be someone they knew and trusted—
There is a killer among us, and it could be my neighbor.

AT the viewing, Anita reflected back on the short, sweet
life of Peter. She smiled softly to herself as she recalled
that sometimes, he called his mother "Wayne," since that
was as close as he could come to pronouncing "Elaine."
When Elaine turned thirty, Peter carried a sign around the
town square and into his mother's office at Davenport Office Supply. Anyone who knew the family laughed as soon
as they read, "My mommy is 30 today. Happy Birthday
Wayne!"

Anita's eyes focused back on the tiny body in front of
her and no longer could see that little boy. "He looked like
a very old person who had abused his life and body to the
maximum. He did not look like a three-and-a-half-year-old.
Whatever [the killer] did to the child that night, he stripped
him of every feeling and emotion. Whatever innocence was
in that three-and-a-half-year-old was gone."

Joann Settle remembered her former tenants as a likeable, friendly couple. They were very active in the community and in the small church, where Elaine played the
piano and Keith led the singing. Her favorite memory of
the family was Halloween, 1996, at the Fall Festival in Ina.
One of the highlights of that celebration is the annual costume competition. The multi-talented Elaine had created a
trio of costumes that year based on *The Wizard of Oz*. Keith
was decked out as the Tin Man, Peter as the Cowardly Lion
and Elaine, the Scarecrow. Her efforts were rewarded with
the "Best Costume" ribbon that year.

IN the immediate aftermath of the massacre, thirty diligent
local and state detectives delved into this perplexing puzzle.
They interviewed hundreds of people, but a suspect never
surfaced. Their tools were so limited: no money was stolen,
a VCR and portable movie camera were left in plain view,
no evidence pointed to a specific perpetrator; no reason
existed for this quiet and conservative family to have be-

come victims; no one who was questioned recalled anything suspicious.

All they had was a dead family. A mother and father
so devoted to their little boy that they never allowed a mile-
stone to pass without a video camera recording it for pos-
terity. A couple so eager for the birth of their second child
that they wrapped a present for Peter's third birthday with
a card attached reading: "Happy Birthday, big brother, from
January 10th."

And a baseball bat, the one Keith had bought for Peter.
It had been far too big for him, but Keith knew the little
boy would grow into it one day. In the meantime, he could
demonstrate how to hit the ball. One day, Keith dreamed,
they could play ball together.

OVER the years, Joeann Dardeen never gave up searching
for the killer of her son and his family. She gathered more
than 3,000 signatures in her community in 1994 and sent
them to Oprah Winfrey. The producers there were not interested—the crime was too gruesome for television.

Other TV producers were reluctant to present the story
when there were not enough details to assemble a profile
and no suspect to pinpoint. *America's Most Wanted* responded in a similar fashion that year, but in 1998, that
program's producers had a change of heart. Joeann Dardeen
pinned her hopes and her heart on this show's remarkable
success record for closing cases and bringing perpetrators
to justice. But the show that aired in November of that year
produced no suspects, no credible leads. The waiting game
continued.

CHAPTER FOURTEEN

WANTING to leave the area quickly, Sells took a job with a Cape Girardeau, Missouri, company, R. B. Patasnic. They were looking for men to work construction on the two-lane State Road 84 in Florida, known locally as Alligator Alley. When completed, it was renamed Interstate 75, a straight-shot highway running from the Altantic Coast to the Gulf Coast through the lonely wildness of the Everglades.

While Tommy Sells was working in Florida, William Sells, his legal father, died. His passing went unnoticed by his son. One day, hip-deep in the murky water, holding a measure rod, Sells stood breathless as a snake swam past his legs. That was it. That was not the kind of risk he was willing to take. He was out of there.

He returned to St. Louis where he was once again arrested for stealing a motor vehicle on January 13.

In September of 1988, he headed north. That same month, an 11-year-old Salem, New Hampshire, girl, Melissa Ann Trembley, disappeared. She was last seen in a convenience store parking lot talking to a dark-haired man in need of a shave, who sat in the front seat of a rusted tan van.

Her body was found face down on the railroad tracks between two trains at a Boston and Maine freight terminal in Lawrence, Massachusetts, on September 12. She'd suffered sexual assault before being stabbed to death. Footprints and blood, sixty-five feet from where her body was discovered, indicated that she'd struggled with her attacker.

To add insult to this discarded victim, a slow-moving

freight train being pulled into the terminal rolled over her body, further desecrating it where she lay.

IN Salt Lake City, Utah, that fall, a woman with a 3-year-old son fell under the spell of Tommy Lynn Sells. He put them to work on the streets by his side holding a sign that said, "Homeless and hungry. Please help." He coached the little boy to make sad faces and even sadder little smiles. After a few weeks of panhandling, it was time for a road trip. They all piled into a stolen black Dodge van and headed to Idaho to spend the night along the majestic Snake River in Gooding County. Mother and son never returned from that trip. Sells confessed that he'd killed them both and dumped their bodies in the river. He walked away, his pockets still bulging with the cash he'd accumulated from passersby who took pity on a woman and small child.

THE warmth of Tucson drew Tommy Lynn Sells south. There in mid-December he crossed paths with another homeless man, Kent Alan Lauten, a native of Phoenix who bounced back and forth between the two cities.

Sells sold Kent a bag of pot. Kent took the bag and promised to give him money later that day. When they met again, Kent hurled insults at Sells, refusing to pay for his marijuana, taunting him that there was nothing Sells could do about it.

Sells threw a punch that knocked Kent to the ground. Lauten's friends moved in. "Chump" they called him as they threatened Sells. Nothing angered Sells more than being treated with disrespect, but, knowing he was outnumbered, he retreated. He couldn't settle the score that moment, but he knew where Lauten slept.

That night, Sells crept up on his prey. He found him in the arms of a man. As quick as a snake strike, Sells was on top of Kent, a pocketknife in hand. The other man scurried from the scene into the darkness. Kent looked into the eyes of his killer. Then the knife stabbed again and again and streaked across his neck. Kent bled to death—homeless and alone like a dog scavenging the city dump.

With his pocketknife and his bare hands, Sells scratched a shallow indentation in the ground and rolled the body into the makeshift grave. He scattered the paltry pile of dirt from the excavation over it. Then, he piled dead leaves and other debris on top, covered it all with a tarp and tamped it down with his feet.

Sells slunk off into the night and slept.

Two days later, on December 18, a 12-year-old boy wandered into the transient camp seeking a good spot to dig sand for his grandfather. His planned chore flew from his head when he spied a human hand protruding eerily from the ground. By then, Tommy Lynn Sells was in San Bernardino, California.

SELLS was arrested on Christmas Eve for assault with a deadly weapon. Law enforcement was unable to locate the victim and had to release him.

He headed north, on Interstate 5, stopping next in Berkeley. On January 27, 1989, a dispute arose between him and a ticket agent at a BART train station. It generated a report that established Sells' presence in the area.

Sells claimed he was responsible for the death of a 20-year-old prostitute while there. According to his story, it was a drug deal gone bad. He had originally thought he was bargaining with a man, but discovered her gender shortly before he killed her. Police found an unidentified body around that time where he claimed to have left hers, just north of Lake Tahoe in a town called Truckee.

SELLS made a side trip to Colorado in March, then continued north on Route 5 until he reached Roseburg, Oregon, a small town along the interstate, an hour south of Eugene. He worked for a mom-and-pop woodcutting business, and lived at the home of a local couple.

He spent his workdays chasing chokers up and down the mountainside and chopping the felled trees into firewood for his employer's roadside stand.

While in the area, Sells said, he'd kidnapped a long-haired young girl in her twenties, and raped and killed her. On May 9, he met a hitchhiker who wanted to go to Washington State with him. But when she tried to steal his dope, he murdered her, too. He left both bodies in the forest where he cut trees. Later that same day, he was arrested for second-degree theft for dipping his hand in the kitty at the firewood stand and pulling out $30.

After serving fifteen days in the Roseburg jail, Tommy Lynn Sells was a free man again.

HE made a short stop in Berkeley before making his journey east to Arkansas. On August 16, 1989, he was charged with theft by receiving and arrested in North Little Rock. On the 23rd of that month, the charges were dropped and Sells was footloose once more.

He bounced back to Oakland briefly, then detoured up to Montana for a short visit with a girlfriend in Missoula.

Then, it was back to Oakland, just in time to experience the earthquake of October 17. Shortly before it struck, Sells disembarked from the commuter train and went into a restroom to shoot up heroin. He was standing just outside the facilities with a pocket rocket of Night Train pressed firmly to his lips when the tremors hit and the lights went out. He grabbed a light pole and hung on. At first, he was certain he was experiencing the negative side effects of his drug and alcohol abuse. Then, he noticed the light pole swaying back and forth and heard the sound of buildings and roads collapsing.

Sells didn't wait for the aftershocks. He raced south to Reno. The next night, he was arrested and put into a detox center.

Once again, rehabilitation was a wasted effort. He was arrested in Carson City, Nevada, and yet another rehab center housed him for an additional thirty days. In December of that year, he overdosed on heroin and was hospitalized in Phoenix for forty-eight hours.

In January 1990, Sells returned to Salt Lake City. On

the 7th, he was arrested for possession of cocaine and for vehicle burglary. When the crime lab results showed that the substance was not cocaine, he was released. He shuffled off to Wyoming. His activities there would earn him an extended stay in prison.

CHAPTER FIFTEEN

In Rawlins, Wyoming, on January 12, 1990, Sells struck up a conversation with a young couple, both about 18. The woman was in the late stages of pregnancy. The tires on their truck were as bald as a baby's head. Sells offered to help them out with their transportation problem.

He prowled around the area until he found a 1978 Dodge four-wheel-drive pick-up with the right size tires. Then, he stole it.

Bobby Daniels bolted out of his house in pursuit of his runaway vehicle. When it drove out of sight, Daniels returned to the house where he and Athena Davis lived and called 9-1-1 to report the theft.

Sells removed the tires from the stolen pick-up and put them on the desperate couple's truck. Taking a duffle bag out of its interior, Sells abandoned the tire-stripped truck and went in search of alternate transportation.

As Bobby and Athena described the man in the green shirt and red hat they had seen shortly before the truck was stolen, Tony Selzer was protecting his pick-up from certain theft. He confronted a similarly dressed man carrying a dark duffle bag when he caught him climbing into his truck. Sells made a hasty retreat, ditching the duffle on his way.

Police spotted the young pair's truck, with the hot, nearly new tires, in no time. They told their tale and offered yet a third, corroborating description of the truck thief.

Sells hid, four blocks from the scene of the crime, waiting for a train to glide through and give him a ride out of town. One hour after the truck theft, he ran out to jump a freight car. Officer David Anderson saw him before he made his getaway, and arrested him for public intoxication.

He was held on $10,000 bond once the car theft charge came to light. Deeming him indigent, the Carbon County judge appointed John Hoke as public defender. The case was bound over to the court for the Second Judicial District.

On February 2, Hoke filed a motion to suspend further proceeds until the accused could be examined for any mental illness or deficiency. The court complied, ordering Sells to be transported to the Wyoming State Hospital.

The medical personnel there were given thirty days to assess and evaluate Sells' mental condition and file a written report about any mental illness or deficiency, his capacity to comprehend the nature of the proceedings and his ability to conform his conduct to the requirements of the law.

On arrival at the Wyoming State Hospital, admitting physician Dr. Howard Winkler described him as "[. . .] a well-developed, well-nourished, twenty-five-year-old white male who looks very much like Charles Manson with heavy, unkempt black beard, long shoulder length brownish-black hair. [. . .] He looks dirty and disheveled. [. . .] His mood is flattened."

He further stated that Sells' content of thought was bizarre. "From the tattoos on his arms, he hears the bird, the wolf and the dragon talking to him, telling him to do various things." He concluded that Sells had no recognition of his problems, and that his outlook was poor.

On March 1, Sells requested to be put back on Thorazine, saying, "I'm having problems dealing with things and I don't know if I can handle it." Hospital records indicated that before his arrest he was heavily using alcohol and drugs—cocaine, marijuana, methamphetamines, hallucinogens and heroin, his drug of choice. He was almost continuously intoxicated on one drug or another. Total withdrawal, the records warned, could result in psychosis.

Sells had a history of mood swings over a number of years. His personality was characterized by anti-social, unpredictable and self-destructive behavior. Outbursts of temper would result from minimal provocation. He was easily frustrated and impulsive. He was unable to read and write.

Dr. Peter Heinbecker rendered a diagnosis of depressive disorder; severe opioid, amphetamine, cannabis and alcohol dependency; poly–substance abuse of barbiturates, inhalants and hallucinogens; and a personality disorder with anti-social, borderline and schizoid features. After evaluation, he was prescribed 5 mg Haldol, an anti-psychotic, and 5mg Cogentin, a medicine to control tremors.

Sells returned to the Carbon County jail in early March. In Dr. Heinbecker's official report to Judge Lehman, he wrote, "The defendant maintains the capacity to comprehend his position, to understand the nature and object of the proceedings against him, to conduct his defense in a rational manner, and to cooperate with his counsel to the end that any available defense may be interposed." He concluded, "[. . .] he is presently competent to stand trial, even though mentally ill, and will remain competent in the foreseeable future, even in the absence of any specific treatment for his mental illness."

On March 12, Sells was rushed from jail to the emergency room. He was having shakes and reported, "I feel like I'm bouncing off the walls." He was diagnosed with a severe anxiety attack.

An ambulance raced him to the emergency room again on March 18. Once again, he was shaking, but it was worse than before. His speech was slurred, he had spasms in various muscles and his stuttering was uncontrollable. This time, his medications came under suspicion. They changed his prescriptions to 25 mg Elavil, an anti-depressant, and 80 mg of Inderal SR for hypertension. Later, they enhanced his pharmaceutical soup with the addition of 50, then 100 mg of Mellaril, an anti-psychotic, and 25 mg of Valium for anxiety.

In custody, Sells was a model prisoner. There were no disciplinary actions taken. He completed the 265-hour course in "Professional Barber-Styling." He worked in the leather shop and as an outside trustee at the Wyoming

Honor Conservation Camp, a forestry center. In January 1991, he was released from custody. He wandered off again, first to Colorado and then back east to Florida.

IN Marianna, Florida, on December 9, the Christmas season kicked off with the traditional annual parade. Twenty-five-year-old Teresa Hall was there with her daughter, Tiffany. The 5-year-old clapped her hands, laughed and thoroughly enjoyed the passing musicians and entertainers. Her biggest thrill was Santa Claus.

The little girl was exhausted from the excitement of the evening—ready to sleep with sugarplums dancing in her head. Her eyes were drooping by the time they reached their Village Road home in a semi-wooded rural area in the unincorporated town of Cypress. The railroad tracks that traveled from Jacksonville through the panhandle and out of the state were just one hundred feet from their door. Teresa prepared Tiffany for bed, looking forward to putting her feet up and relaxing a bit after a long day.

Then, their front door was kicked in, exploding dreams of Christmas into a shattered night of violence. The invader raged through their home, knocking obstacles out of his way. He lifted a table over his head and smashed it to the floor, splintering it, splitting it in two. He jerked a leg loose and brandished it as he approached Teresa. He bludgeoned her to death with blows that fractured her skull. Then, little Tiffany suffered the same fate. The killer fled the home still clenching the leg of the table in his balled-up fist.

TERESA did not report to work at the New Beginnings Clothing Shop in Marianna the next day. Linda Schack, owner of the store, tried to call her at home. The phone rang unanswered all day, so she called Teresa's mother, Charlotte Mitchell.

Angus Mitchell, Teresa's stepfather, went to check on the family. His heart sank when he saw the damaged door. He entered with great trepidation and discovered the two battered bodies bathed in blood.

A few minutes later, Brian Hall, Teresa's husband and Tiffany's father, returned home from a trip to Quitman, Georgia, where he had worked a carpet-laying job for the last two days. Once Brian's alibi was verified, the police had no suspects and no answers for the bereaved family.

Angel Maturino Resendiz would come under suspicion after his apprehension by Texas Rangers in 2000. Resendiz, dubbed "the Railway Killer," had been linked to a string of murders occurring near railroad tracks across the south. Sells admitted committing the crimes; authorities, although suspicious, are uncertain.

ON March 14, 1992, Tommy Lynn Sells was arrested in Charleston, South Carolina, for public drunkenness. He received a thirty-day suspended sentence. On April 2, he was arrested again on the same charge. As soon as he was released, he left town. The mountains of West Virginia would next embrace Sells. Their rugged, primitive beauty fueled his next act of violence.

CHAPTER SIXTEEN

FABIENNE Witherspoon felt pretty confident of her ability to take care of herself at the age of 20. At five feet, eight inches, with a solid athletic body, she had a physical advantage many women lacked. Her attractive, oval-shaped face, with dark brown, nearly black eyes, had just enough of an edge of toughness that no one could ever accuse her of being cute. Thick, curly brown hair fell below her shoulders, its uninhibited style suggesting a streak of wildness lying just beneath the surface.

On the 13th of May, she was house-sitting at 906 Grove Avenue in Charleston, West Virginia. It was an ordinary middle-class neighborhood where bad things normally did not happen. That day, she had only one worry on her mind as she walked a few blocks to the Women's Health Clinic for a pregnancy test.

On her stroll back to the house she was feeling benevolent toward the world, relieved at the negative result of her test. She saw a man in his mid-twenties with uncombed, matted hair, intriguing eyes and scruffy clothing at the corner of Washington Street and Pennsylvania Avenue. He held a sign that read, "Hungry. Will work for food."

He spun a tale of misery and woe in a softly beguiling voice with a barely Southern accent. Below his plea for pity lurked a scintilla of dangerous flirtation. He told her his name was Tommy Sells. He said that he and his wife lived under a bridge, and his children were so very hungry. A wave of compassion welled up in Fabienne, tinged with a drop of sexual attraction. She brought him to her home to scrounge up what she could. Once there, she grabbed two black trash bags. Into one, she threw graham crackers, Cheerios, scalloped potato mix, vanilla wafers and more until the bag bulged. Into the other, she stuffed folded, clean clothing. She smiled at him and asked if he needed anything else.

"My wife really needs some underwear," he said.

Fabienne went into the back bedroom to find a few pair. As she turned from the chest of drawers, there he was, right behind her. And in his hand was a knife from her kitchen. Her gullibility gleamed on its blade.

Sells brought the knife to her throat. "Take off your clothes," he demanded.

She hesitated, but the cold blade of the knife under her chin jerked her into action. With fumbling fingers, she removed her shirt and unfastened her bra. She kicked off her shoes and pushed off her socks with the toes of her opposite foot. She reached for the waistband of her pants, and froze.

Sells clenched the knife between his teeth, pushed her hands away and pulled down her pants. As soon as he started to remove his clothing, Fabienne's eyes looked away, riveting to the floor. Then, he shoved, smacked and threatened her into the bathroom and down to her knees. At the point of the knife, she took him into her mouth.

He pushed her back on the floor, spread her legs and penetrated her vaginally. Fabienne just lay there, praying he would finish, just finish and leave her alone—wondering all the while how she could have been so stupid.

He stopped, rose to his feet and ordered her into the shower. There, he inserted his fingers inside her, making her wince. Then he brutally penetrated her again.

He shoved her out of the shower and onto her knees, once more demanding oral sex. Please, please let this end, she thought.

He jerked her toward the toilet and made her bend over. She felt the pressure of the head of his penis against her anus. She spotted a ceramic duck on the back of the commode, and, grabbing it, smashed it into his head. Shards of duck flew around the bathroom and she pummeled him again and again with the remains of the figurine.

In the struggle, she got a hand on the knife and wrested it out of Sells' control. She stumbled out of the bathroom and toward the front door. But, he was on her again, manhandling her into the bedroom. She stabbed him. He grabbed her wrist and regained possession of the knife, jabbing at her. She jumped back and received a deep slice across her skin, but now, she was in control of the knife.

They wrestled through the bedroom, alternating control and exchanging stabs, cuts and blows. Finally, he got her down on the floor and got on top of her. He strapped her wrists and ankles together with Scotch tape. Then he secured the bindings by tying strips of sheets he ripped from the bed over the tape.

He raised an antique piano stool over his head and beat her scalp and body without mercy. The blows were so hard, the seat broke loose from its base. He made a half-hearted attempt to slit her throat, but by this time, he was in a panic. The cut he inflicted there only required three stitches.

He grabbed a VCR and a boom-box and made his escape. He left behind the gifts of compassion, an overflowing bag of clothing and an equally stuffed bag of food.

As soon as Fabienne regained consciousness from the blow to her head, she fought her way out of her bonds. She wrapped herself in a blanket, picked up her portable phone and rushed outside, trailing Scotch tape in her wake.

She called 9-1-1. Her descent down her front steps left a trail of dripping blood and crumpled tape.

"I have never seen a person alive with so much blood on her," said Sergeant Richard Westfall of the Charleston Police Department.

Before leaving in the ambulance, Fabienne told investigators that the man who had assaulted her was Tommy Sells and that he slept by the river.

Sgt. Westfall processed the crime scene with Detective H. S. Walker while Detective Rollins and Lieutenant Epperhart searched the riverbank for suspects. Sells was not an unknown quantity to the criminal investigation division. He had been observed for four or five weeks holding a sign at the corner of Quarrier and Clendenin Streets. In a short time, Detective Carl Hammons had an address for their suspect. He and Westfall went to 833A Bigley Avenue and questioned Sells' former roommates, Curtis Sizemore, Rebecca Gibson and Karin Pamela Young.

When the officers initiated the questioning, they were certain that they were talking to one man and two women. They were wrong. Karin Young was not a woman. By the end of the interview, they knew. Karin was a transvestite whose transformation was so complete and convincing, he fooled two men with extensive vice experience.

When Sells had first met Karin, he was deceived as well. So much so that the first time he was intimate with Karin's sister, Gina, he had a moment of doubt about her, too. "I'm going to put my hand down your pants, and if I find anything there that shouldn't be, I'll kill you," he'd told her. He said it was a joke. He said Gina thought it was very funny.

Curtis, Rebecca and Karin told the investigators that Sells had come to the apartment about 5 o'clock. He told them he was bleeding from a fight, but was not going to go to the hospital. While there, he had removed his shirt and stuffed it in a garbage bag. Westfall retrieved the shirt and bagged it as evidence.

When asked if they knew where Sells had gone, Curtis volunteered that he had taken him to the place where Sells had been living for the past week. It was the apartment of his girlfriend's daughter and Karin's sister, Gina Young.

AFTER arriving at Gina's place, Sells called his mother to ask her how to butterfly a cut. She asked, "What kind of cut?"

"Oh, a cut here and a cut there."

"How many cuts?" she insisted.

He held the receiver to his chest and turned to his girlfriend, "Gina, Mom wants to know how many."

Gina looked him over and counted a total of twenty-three, but a few of those were only superficial wounds. Sells' mother explained how to bandage his injuries and told him to get to a hospital. Instead of seeking medical attention, he sent Gina out to buy a fifth of Jim Beam and score some dope.

When she came back from her mission, Sells was dripping with fatalistic self-pity. "Gina, if I die, make sure I get back to Missouri."

An hour later, Detective Hammons and Sergeant Westfall arrived at the door of Apartment #4, 303 South Ranch Road in Elkview. Gina stepped back from the doorway and allowed the officers to enter. They found Sells lying on the living room floor in obvious pain, with multiple stab wounds to his abdomen. His external bleeding was minimal, but internally it was profuse. His spleen and kidney were nicked, a lung was partially collapsed and his testicles were sliced. The detectives called for an ambulance and rushed him to Charleston General Hospital for trauma surgery and a week-long stay.

INITIALLY, the case appeared cut and dried, but when prosecutors prepared for trial, problems arose. It had not been long since Fabienne had filed another sexual assault charge that was never prosecuted. To the jury, the questionable nature of that charge could cast doubt on her current claim. To make matters worse, the defense uncovered psychological reports that reflected poorly on the victim. They threatened to use this information in court in defense of their client.

In light of these revelations, the prosecution was no longer confident it could find Sells guilty and put him behind bars in a jury trial. They were ready to deal with the defense. Some jail time, they reasoned, was better than the chance of none at all. The two sides agreed on a plea bargain. The sexual assault charges were dropped. On June 25, 1993, Judge Tod J. Kaufman sentenced Sells to "an indeterminate term of not less than two years and not more than

ten years" for malicious wounding. The judge gave him
credit for four hundred and two days' time already served.
He was housed in the Northern Correctional Facility in
Moundsville, West Virginia, just south of Wheeling.

SELLS had one friend waiting for him behind bars: Billy
Young, Gina's heterosexual brother. Young watched Sells
back from the moment the cell door clicked behind him
until Sells left that facility.

Sells started out his term as a model prisoner, earning
the designation of trustee. He soon abused that position,
though. He and another inmate named Gregory Carter
found a .357 pistol on the inside. They planned to trade it
for dope. For safekeeping until then, Sells hid the weapon
in the warden's office. Another trustee caught him in the
act and reported him. Charges were filed and then dropped
when Sells was moved to maximum security at Mt. Olive
Prison.

This time, while in prison in West Virginia, Sells
taught himself to read with the help of a Bible. "I could
not read 'Run, Dick, run; run, Jane, run' when I quit the
ninth grade at the age of sixteen," he admitted. He worked
hard at his self-education, pushing himself to reach his
goal—sending the first letter of his life.

In 1994, Sells struck up a friendship with a newly arrived inmate, John Price. Price was a nurse who had been
working for a home health service company based in Lo-
gan, West Virginia. Three of his friends were found dead
after injections of Dilaudid, a morphine-based prescription
drug that is ten to one hundred times as powerful as street
heroin. It was without doubt that he was the source of the
drug, but evidence of a more active role in their demise
was weak. Facing the possibility of a life sentence, Price
pled guilty to providing the drug and paraphernalia, but
denied having administered the injections. He was behind
bars for causing their deaths.

He told Sells about his sister, Nora. She was 26 years
old, a bit slow and childlike—a product of special educa-

tion classes in the public school system. Most importantly, she got an SSI check every month. She often visited her brother and he introduced her to Sells.

TERRY and Crystal Harris packed up their belongings, loaded up their four kids and moved to the Del Rio area in 1995. Just two days after their arrival in West Texas, the couple was married in a quiet ceremony.

As soon as the vows were spoken and sealed with a kiss, Terry set the wheels in motion to keep his promise to Katy. He filed adoption papers for all three of Crystal's children. The paperwork culminated in a family trip to the courthouse. When they emerged, Terry Harris was the legal father of all of them. The children formed a ring around their parents and burst into song: "We are the Harrises! We are the Harrises! Hooray! Hooray! Hooray! We are the Harrises! We are the Harrises! Forever more today!"

DURING her first visits with Sells, Nora Price sat on her side of the glass with a telephone receiver pressed to her ear. The cold barrier, the stale smell and the close proximity of other visitors did not create a very romantic ambiance. But romance sprung from this infertile ground nonetheless and wound its way around this simple woman's heart. Later, contact visits enriched the encounters and sealed Nora's fate.

Sells took advantage of the pretty girl's intellectual deficiency. He sweet-talked Nora into falling in love with him. She was an easy mark. She'd had a rough, unhappy life and could not recall anyone ever being so nice to her. They talked and wrote about the day he would get out of jail and about all of the things they could do together. He conned her out of small amounts of cash for months. Then he moved in for the kill.

He informally proposed to her by letter. Then came the big day. Mt. Olive Prison had an annual event where visitors can have a whole day with the prisoners.

Out on the prison lawn, on a lovely spring day with

the sun caressing their skin, Tommy asked, "You want to get married?"

The warmth of the mellow sun competed with the warmth in Nora's heart. She thought this was the most wonderful moment of her life. While still in prison, in April of 1996, Tommy Lynn Sells married Nora Price. From that day on, three-quarters of Nora's SSI checks poured into Sells' coffers at prison.

In her honor, Sells got two tattoos with "Nora" written into their design. One was a rose on his neck. The other was a Harley-Davidson with a dragon on his right upper arm. Nora was delighted.

In his time at this facility, mental health professionals diagnosed Sells as bi-polar. His illness went untreated. He was released into an unsuspecting world in May of 1997.

CHAPTER SEVENTEEN

WITHIN days of his release, Tommy Sells left Nora behind in West Virginia. On June 1, he called her from Michigan and told her he wanted to get back together. She agreed, and he returned to West Virginia. Together they hit the road, hitchhiking and riding trains to Tennessee. They settled in the town of Cleveland at #2 Sunset Trail. Sells got a job at a car wash. On July 29, local police gave him a ticket for driving without a license.

Sells abandoned Nora in Tennessee on August 18 and headed west. Nora, unable or unwilling to cope on her own, dragged her empty, broken heart back to her home state, West Virginia.

On September 5, from Oregon Sells called his mother in St. Louis and Nora's mother in Spurlockville, West Virginia. He traveled back east, retrieved Nora from the Mountain State and took her to his mother's home in Missouri. By this time, Nora was pregnant.

In October, Sells got a mechanic's job at 360 Degree Auto. He stayed off drugs for three weeks. The family had high hopes that Tommy was going to settle down at last. But neither one of the women nor his job could keep Sells drug-free. "He came home one night higher than Georgia pine," his mother said. In no time, tracks covered his arms.

Nothing could keep Sells tied to home. By mid-October, he was stalking fresh prey.

SELLS privately admitted to the murder of Joel Kirkpatrick. He has never confessed to authorities and no one has undertaken an investigation into his possible involvement.

The following is a combination of the facts of the crime and the details provided by Tommy Lynn Sells.

Sells traveled east of St. Louis on Interstate 64. An exit onto Route 50 sent him straight across Illinois to Lawrenceville near the Indiana border. Near this small town, October 13, 1997, felt like any other uneventful fall day. But shortly after 4 a.m., it would brand itself into the community's collective memory.

Sells first met Julie Rea at a convenience store where, he said, she had treated him rudely. From that moment on, Sells was consumed with a desire for revenge.

Anger drove him, fed him, led him straight to the front door of a house he'd never entered before. With great care, he broke the window, making no more noise than if he had crumpled up a sheet of cellophane. He slid toward the kitchen—such a wonderful place for a predator; always a weapon in easy reach. He picked up a knife and weighed its balance in his hand. He headed straight for the first bedroom door. There, 10-year-old Joel Kirkpatrick dreamed his last dream.

Sells plunged the knife into Joel's body, oblivious to the blood that splattered in his face and on his clothes. A scream pierced the quiet of Julie Rea's home. It slapped her awake and lifted her out of bed.

The killer left his victim lying at the foot of the bed and slipped from the boy's room and away from the approaching woman. She raced up the hall to her son. "Joel? Joel?"

She looked through the doorway of the dark room and saw an empty bed. She turned from the room, frantic. That is when she spotted him. The hood of his sweatshirt was pulled up and the drawstring tightened across his face concealing his features.

She ran toward him, her personal safety irrelevant in the face of her fear for her son. She grappled with him briefly until he pushed her off and headed toward the back of the house. She chased him through the glass doors and into the backyard, screaming inarticulate pleas for help.

Outside, Julie tripped over an insignificant obstruction,

invisible in the night, and fell face first on the ground. The intruder doubled back, hitting her in the head, hoping to delay her pursuit.

She was too dazed to move—or even to think for a brief moment. Then, she raised herself on her arms and saw the fleeing man again. He pulled the hood down, revealing his face under a streetlight.

She jumped to her feet, torn between chasing after him and running for help. She chose the latter and rushed to Lesa Bridgett's house on the other side of the street and pounded on the door. Once inside, she called the police and reported her son's abduction.

In minutes, officers were on the scene. They found 10-year-old Joel Kirkpatrick in his bedroom. His small body was crumpled like a discarded tissue used to stanch a bloody nose. He was clothed in a blood-drenched tee shirt. The shirt was marred by a multitude of angry stab wounds.

His mother, Julie, was taken to the emergency room with a black eye, scratches and abrasions on the tops of her feet, her knees and inside her legs, wounds on both shoulders, internal bruising and a laceration on her right arm requiring five sutures.

CHAPTER EIGHTEEN

TOMMY Lynn Sells was on the move, headed for Springfield, Missouri.

As he haunted its streets, a young brown-haired woman captured his attention. He followed her, watching and waiting—waiting for the moment he could lure her from her safe world and into his. Unfruitful stalking drove Sells' to a fever pitch.

From his vantage point in his parked van, he sought a more vulnerable target. He saw a man and three children enter an apartment. The oldest child was 13 years old, with auburn hair, a freckled nose and a toothy grin. Her name was Stephanie Mahaney. Sells turned his focus and his fantasies to the potential victim in that apartment.

Suzette Carlisle, the mother of these children, was not at home. She had been admitted to the hospital with a life-threatening bout of pneumonia. Her fiancé, Rob Martin, had brought the children to the hospital to visit her that night. Upon returning home, he played video games with them and stayed in the apartment on North Robberson until all the children were asleep. Stephanie was so tired, she collapsed on the bed in a long gray tee shirt with a full-length Bugs Bunny on the front.

At 11 o'clock, Sells saw the man leave by the back door, locking it behind him before returning to sit by Suzette's side. Rob had assumed the front door was locked, since it was rarely used.

Sells crept through the night as silent as an alley cat intent on its hunt for an unsuspecting mouse. He slipped through the front door into the quiet home. He went room to room seeking his next victim. He looked in on the 8-year-old and the 9-year-old. Then he found Stephanie.

Stephanie's eyes flew open as a wide piece of tape slapped across her mouth, partially blocking her nose and making it difficult to breathe. Sells jerked her out of bed, dragging her to the front door. With her glasses abandoned on the nightstand, her world was a blur.

She struggled to free herself from his tight grip. She merely made her abductor angrier and the intensity of his hold more painful. He tossed her into the front seat of the van. Whimpering, she lurched toward the door to try to escape.

"Shut up," he said, smashing the back of his hand across her face.

They drove into the countryside. Stephanie was afraid to make another attempt at escape. Afraid to leap from a moving van. Afraid to stay where she was. But every time she mounted the courage to make a move to freedom, she was smacked back into the seat.

Finally, Sells parked just off of Missouri 266 on Greene County Farm Road 99. He turned onto a road that was not much more than a path through a field. He swung open a gate that blocked his path and drove into the cow pasture. To make Stephanie more malleable, he injected her with a large dose of cocaine. He forced off her underpants, hitting her in the face whenever she struggled. She cringed when his hand moved toward her face again. He grabbed the edge of the tape and ripped it off her face in one swift movement, bringing tears to her eyes. Putting his hand behind her head, he pushed her down to penetrate her mouth. Then, he raped her. When he was through, he pressed down on her, his hands enclosed around her throat. He squeezed tightly, his arms shaking with the effort. Beneath him, her arms and legs twitched, her torso bucked. His fingers turned white as he applied the pressure for five long minutes. First, Stephanie lost consciousness—and then she lost her life.

He gathered up the girl's discarded underwear and her abused body and walked toward the bucolic farm pond. There he dropped her body into the water like unwanted trash into a garbage chute. He sluiced the cleansing wetness over his sweaty face, shook his head and drove away.

Rob Martin returned to the apartment at 5:30 the next morning. He'd planned to make breakfast for the three children and make sure they got to school on time. He unlocked the back door and heard the sound of an alarm clock. He went into Stephanie's room to shut it off and coax her out of bed. She was not there. He checked on the other two children. They were both sound asleep. He looked in every room. He called out her name. He woke the other two and questioned them. Stephanie was nowhere to be found.

Within hours, Suzette filed a missing persons report. She did not believe her daughter had run away. Stephanie was a real homebody. She took care of her younger siblings like a mother hen—her developing maternal instincts at an all-time high in the face of her mother's serious illness. Instead of running around with her friends, she was more likely to sit with them on the front porch engaged in hours of conversation. For a thirteen-year-old, she was very responsible. At the time, though, Stephanie was one of twenty-six runaway or missing girls reported in the area.

In the weeks that followed her disappearance, investigators talked to more than thirty people and searched six homes. They were unable to confirm any of the reported sightings of the young girl.

Thirty-four days passed with no word of Stephanie. Then, on Tuesday, November 18, 1997, a group of hunters wandering through a field discovered the partially clothed body of a young teenaged girl submerged in the pond. When investigators arrived at the scene, they found a pair of jeans and one shoe nearby.

The body was too decomposed to make visual identification possible. Greene County Sheriff's Department detectives called all twenty-six families of missing girls to inform them of their discovery, and to obtain dental records and refine any descriptions they had on file.

LATE Wednesday, November 19, 1997, the unknown body had a name—Stephanie Mahaney. The Greene County Medical Examiner, James Spindler, identified her through her dental records and a birthmark on her right ear.

Information about her disappearance was sparse. Investigators received only fifteen calls reporting tips after the body was found—an all-time low. Twenty members of the Green County Sheriff's Department and volunteer high school Explorer Scouts returned to the scene for a grid-by-grid search.

Wrapped up warmly against the cold and wind, they marched in a determined line, halting the moment someone shouted, "Stop!" Once the found item was bagged as possible evidence, the line moved forward.

On Christmas Eve, the results of the autopsy were made public. The decompression of the tissues in her throat showed that Stephanie had died of strangulation. Additionally, signs of trauma were noted on the face. Decomposition was too far advanced to determine whether or not a sexual assault had occurred.

A picture of Stephanie became a permanent fixture on the bulletin board of one detective, Jim Arnott. It was the only unsolved murder in twenty years or more in Greene County. He also carried a picture of her in his notebook and another in his car. He never stopped thinking about what had happened to Stephanie Mahaney.

SELLS, however, had brushed the memories of that night right out of his mind. He returned to his mother and wife in St. Louis and continued working at the same auto shop until he took off again.

On December 15, he was back in Winnemucca, Nevada, but he stayed just one night, at the Overland Hotel. Before leaving the area, he drove out to the desolate spot where he'd left Stefanie Stroh's body in 1987—reliving his fond memories of that fatal night. He was back in St. Louis in time to get another traffic ticket on December 29, 1997. That day he left town and Nora never saw the father of her unborn child again.

Sells was not happy when he left St. Louis. Nora would give birth to his progeny in three months' time. He did not feel equipped or inclined to take care of a wife and a baby. He had hoped his younger brother, Randy, would raise the child. But Randy did not really want any children. He feared, too, that if he took in Tommy's child, his brother would be hitting him up for cash and favors constantly.

Nina knew that Nora did not have the ability to care for a child on her own, and Tommy was not responsible or stable enough to help. At her age, she did not feel capable of raising any child—not even her own grandchild. With the help of a sister in Jonesboro, Arkansas, she contacted an attorney to arrange for an adoption. He came to her home with a schoolteacher to evaluate Nora and to be certain she did want to give up her baby.

In April 1998, in a hospital in Jonesboro, Nora gave birth to a baby boy by caesarean section. She never saw her child. He was immediately placed with a family in that town, where he lived for the next four years.

Nina was determined not to have to go through this ordeal one more time. "To keep Nora from getting pregnant again, Nina had her get fixed," Sells said.

Nora returned to St. Louis to live with her mother-in-law. Sells was nowhere near Jonesboro when his son was born. He had pawned his mechanic's tools in Little Rock, Arkansas, on January 19, 1998, and traveled south.

CHAPTER NINETEEN

CARNIVAL season started early every year in South Texas—1998 was not an exception. Sells hooked up with the Heart of America outfit in Aransas Pass. He drove the truck that hauled the Ferris wheel, and also operated the ride. The carnival moved from town to town down Highway 90 as it runs west from San Antonio to the border. On the way, it passed a multitude of small towns like Castroville, a community of dramatic hills and valleys founded by immigrants from the Alsace–Lorraine region between Germany and France. Then they rolled through Hondo, a town with an Old West feel and a road sign that read, "Hondo is a little bit of heaven so don't drive through it like hell." Farther along they hit Knippa, a tiny town with a welcome sign that reassured all drivers passing through: "You can go ahead and blink. Knippa's bigger than you think." The last town they cut through on Route 90 was Uvalde, a quaint county seat with an inviting old-fashioned town square dominated by the no-nonsense architecture of its old courthouse.

After Uvalde, the carnival caravan headed south to La Pryor, then west again before coming to the scruffy border town of Eagle Pass, best known for a history of bizarrely crooked politicians. Across the Rio Grande is Piedras Negras, Mexico. Eagle Pass residents cross this border whenever they want a more elegant night on the town than Pizza Hut can offer. After a two-week stint there, the nomadic troupe moved north to Del Rio, a border town with a bit more polish than its southern neighbor. Del Rio and Ciudad Acuña strut their cultural diversity in unison with joint promotional materials for tourists. Another influence in the shaping of this small city of 34,000 is Laughlin Air Force Base.

THE second week the carnival was in town, on the evening of March 5, 1998, Jessica Levrie brought her children to the bright lights and rides. It was an unusually cool night for March in this part of the country. While the kids rode the Ferris wheel, she stood on the sidelines enjoying their squeals and smiles. The green eyes and open, welcoming face of this Hispanic woman caught the interest of Tommy Lynn Sells.

"Wouldn't it be a nice night for a cup of cocoa?" he asked.

The children disembarked the ride and begged to go around again. While they soared back into the air, Jessica invited the ride operator to her home for a warm cup. Sells ended up spending that night and subsequent ones at her home while he finished up his run in Del Rio. On the day the carnival packed up to leave, Jessica popped in and out of the grounds, grabbing a word here and there with Tommy as he worked with the crew preparing to travel.

Tommy sat in the rig in the parking lot ready to go—just waiting for the signal to roll out. Jessica showed up one more time. He was smitten by her beauty and her sense of style, but most of all, he was rocked by the love that emanated from her like heat from a campfire on a cold and dreary night.

"Do you want to ride with me to Corpus Christi?" he asked her.

A grin split her face and her head bobbled "yes." She hopped in the truck for the fourteen-hour drive to the Gulf Coast.

Jessica spent two days in the seaside city. Then, Tommy put her on a bus back home to Del Rio. She returned in her Olds '88 two days later.

With her hands on her hips, she looked Tommy in the eye and said, "Well, are you ready to come home?"

Home was a magic word to this rootless man. The word embodied everything he had missed in life. He clutched it to his heart and accepted her offer.

They traveled back in her car and began living together with Jessica's two teenaged daughters and two younger boys in Del Rio. On March 31, Sells reported to the local unemployment office looking for a job.

And he got one—working as a mechanic and salesman at Amigo Auto Sales. Jessica worked at a Chinese restaurant waiting tables. In his spare time, he drew pictures of roses for Jessica—he loved roses and their intricate beauty, because they reminded him of her. Just a few short years after learning to read and write, he penned love poems to Jessica pouring out his love and devotion.

Following Jessica's lead, he molded and shaped a semblance of a normal life. He and Jessica took turns driving the kids to school. No matter what they tried, the children just could not wake up and get out the door in time to catch the school bus. Tommy took the boys fishing, worked on craft projects with them and occasionally ironed their clothes for school.

Pets were a big part of their family, too. At one point, they had three dogs, two cats, six birds, two hamsters, a guinea pig, a turtle and a snake. For a while, with Jessica's encouragement, Tommy avoided drugs and alcohol and went to work faithfully.

Restless, Sells set off on another road trip on June 28—north to Sonora, Texas, then east to Beaumont. While in northeast Texas, he accumulated two more traffic tickets that were still outstanding a year and a half later when he was arrested for the murder of Kaylene Harris.

Then, he was back home, trying to hang onto the reins of a domestic existence. It only took one family crisis to undo Jessica's good influence and set Sells back on the path he had always traveled.

TWENTY inches of rain fell fast and hard on Del Rio in late August 1998. At 505 Andrade Street in the San Felipe neighborhood, the lights went out. Outside, a woman yelled, filling the air with echoes of her fear. Following the sound of her voice, Virginia Blanco stepped out onto her front porch. The San Felipe Creek had crested its banks and dedicated itself to the destruction of the sad little neighborhood near downtown.

She grabbed a flashlight and pointed its beam catty-corner across the street to the home of her daughter Jessica Levrie. Finally, her shouts and swinging light caught the attention of the family inside.

"C'mon. C'mon over here," Virginia pleaded.

"No, we'll be okay," Jessica replied.

Virginia insisted that her home was safer, and the family relented. Tommy and Jessica stood in the water, passing the four children across the street, one by one. Like a mother hen, Virginia clucked them all safely indoors. Ten minutes later, Virginia opened the front door to discover that the water was already in her yard. Tommy and Jessica joined her on the porch and watched the rising water with a rising sense of dread.

In the street, a woman grabbed for fences, poles and bushes as the water swept her away. Tommy jumped off the porch and tried to save her as she sped past the house. But his clothing snagged on the front-yard fence and the woman slipped away. He pulled only himself to safety.

The raging river running down the street shoved the woman underneath a truck. The motor was running. The truck was full of people hoping to escape the city. Virginia, Tommy and Jessica screamed. They feared that the truck would move and run over her body. A man inside heard their desperate warnings and jumped out of the truck. He struggled through the water and dragged the woman to refuge.

Around the neighborhood, many had already been forced into trees and up on rooftops as liquid fury consumed all in its path. Inside Virginia's house, all four children were put in the room that sat highest above ground level. No one knew at that time, but it was the least safe room in the house.

Water started swirling around Virginia's garage, forming a sluice that swept behind the house and over to an old utility shack. Soon, the shack crashed down and was swept away by the flood.

Unaware of the current state of destruction, Tommy stepped out the front door to get cigarettes from the shop next door owned by Virginia's father. He quickly closed the door and collapsed against it. "It's gone. It's gone," he said, shock etched in his face.

Screams erupted from the back room as the children heard the cries of a trapped cat. At first, they thought it was stuck under the washing machine. But it wasn't there when they looked. Then the horror sunk into their numbed minds. The cat was under the floor, trapped in the rising waters. Tommy grabbed a crowbar and attempted to pull up the boards. The planks would not budge. He beat on them over and over and over again with brutal force. Still, the flooring remained solid. He did not give up while the cat's cries ascended to a crescendo of terror. He did not stop trying until the agonizing screams had faded into the night. His shoulders slumped in defeat. Four pairs of eyes stared at him in disbelief.

The water continued to rise, forcing the children out of the back room. It did not stop rising in the house until it reached the crest of Virginia's hip. Then it rapidly receded, leaving wet and muck in its wake. Virginia's bed sat high and in its center was an oasis of dry. The children lay down there to go to sleep. Exhausted, Virginia collapsed on the soggy sofa and instantly drifted into dreams. Tommy, Jessica and Virginia's 90-year-old father found spots on the soggy floor and settled down in an uneasy peace.

The next morning, the water began to recede, bringing hope to the besieged neighborhood. But around 4 o'clock the next afternoon, Border Patrol went door-to-door, knocking and warning all remaining residents that more water was coming. They transported the sodden survivors to the high school gym. But this shelter was not the refuge they thought it would be. The water rose there as well. All the refugees were evacuated and moved to higher ground at the civic center. Virginia, her father and her daughter's family remained there for two weeks. Authorities then moved the displaced family to the Siesta Motel for a couple of days.

"Then they moved us again. They moved us all over the place," recalled Virginia Blanco.

The flood was a traumatic experience for the whole community. This family was no exception. Looking back on the experience, Sells said, "When I was carrying the kids out of the flood that Jessica and I was in, I knew then nothing, never would be the same again."

Finally, Sells, Jessica and the children found a more permanent place to dwell in a trailer at the American Campgrounds, about ten miles west of Del Rio out past the lake. Soon after they settled in, Tommy and Jessica were driving down Route 90. Tommy abruptly pulled to the side of the road.

"What's wrong, Tommy?" she asked.

"Will you marry me?" he blurted out.

She looked at him in disbelief. He asked her again.

"Are you serious?"

He repeated, "Will you marry me?"

At first she just nodded her head. Then she turned, put a hand on either side of his face and delicately kissed his lips. "Yes, Tommy, I will."

Plans for their wedding raced forward. Jessica Levrie and Tommy Lynn Sells were united in marriage in a Del Rio church on October 22, 1998. Tommy smiled broadly in his rented tux. Jessica beamed in her new burgundy dress. Virginia Blanco, Jessica's brother, her four children and her father were there to share the wedding cake.

In late 1998, Sells worked for several months at Ram Country as a midline mechanic. The aftereffects of the stress from the flood bore down on the newlyweds. Again, Sells was abusing drugs and alcohol, and his working hours became erratic. To Jessica, this behavior was intolerable. Her nagging turned to mutual squabbling. The squabbling escalated to fierce fights. "What Jessica forgot about was, I was doing all this [drinking and drugs] before we met. I just tried to slow down for her. And that was one of our troubles. I should have been doing it for me. I was able to talk to Jessica. She made me feel not afraid. We done everything together when I was at home. Nothing was too good for each other," Sells said.

On February 22, 1999, he left Del Rio. By March 5, he was in Pensacola, Florida. After a phone call to Jessica, he was soon on his way home to Del Rio. He got his job back at Ram Country. But on March 28, she threw him out again, demanding he clean up before he returned. Sells hit the road, hauling a big load of pent-up violence.

CHAPTER TWENTY

JAMIE and Debbie Harris and Debbie's 8-year-old daughter, Ambria Halliburton, moved into a rented trailer in Gibson County, Tennessee in the beginning of January 1999. Their new home was situated in the Caraway Hills area, a sparsely populated community where thick clusters of trees separate neighbors and provide privacy.

By the end of February, marital difficulties drove Jamie and Debbie to separation. All three moved out of the trailer. Jamie moved to the town of Gibson. Debbie thought she had another place to live, but when it did not pan out, she turned to her former landlady, Dawn Patterson. Debbie wanted to move back into the trailer, but she did not have enough money. Dawn agreed to accept her deposit money and allow her to pay the rent a week later. Debbie and Ambria settled back in on March 15.

Dawn last saw Debbie on Monday March 29, when she brought by her rent payment. Debbie was still $25 short and Dawn granted her a few more days. Debbie thanked her and left, saying she was going out for an interview for a second job.

TOMMY Lynn Sells related the events of that night to the Texas Rangers. He said he took a twenty-mile detour north off Route 40 when he reached Jackson, Tennessee. Near midnight on March 30, he approached the quiet trailer. He knocked on the door and it creaked open a crack. He slipped inside. On the counter of the kitchen were a stack of cheerful watermelon-design plates. From the drawer below, he extracted a knife. He slunk down the hallway into

Debbie's bedroom. At the sight of him, a calico cat leaped off the bed and scurried into a hiding place.

He squeezed past the dresser where he was amused to find a price tag bearing the brand name "Tommy." Sitting next to the bed was a makeshift nightstand—an overturned bucket, with an alarm clock and a picture propped on top. He eased himself into the bed and put the blade of the kitchen knife to Debbie's throat.

She did not resist. She did not make a noise. She knew the safety of her daughter depended on this man not knowing Ambria was there. After raping her unresponsive body, Sells stabbed her over and over again.

He stepped across the hallway and into the bathroom, clutching the knife. Setting it down beside the sink, he picked up a bar of soap from a little mouse soap dish and cleaned the blood off his hands and arms.

He turned and looked in the hall. Ambria stood there silently, her face twisted in confusion. He lunged at her and chased her into the living room. When he caught her, he slammed the knife into her small body with the full force of his fury—a thrust with so much power, it lifted her up off her feet. He stabbed her again. She went limp in his grip. He shoved the knife into her again, loosened his grip and she slumped to the floor.

He thought he heard a noise from Debbie's direction, so he returned to the bedroom to make sure she was dead. He thrust the knife into her chest one more time and left it there.

For days, neighbors noticed that Debbie Harris' blue Chevrolet Beretta appeared to be sitting in the driveway more than usual. The landlady decided not to hassle her tenant when she did not show up with the rest of the rent on Friday, as promised. It was Easter weekend, after all. Holidays often put regular schedules out of whack.

On Easter Sunday, a friend paying a visit to Debbie's trailer opened the door to a strong stench of decomposition. The decay was in such an advanced state, it forced the arriving investigators to tack up a Day-Glo orange sign on the door that read, "Danger. Biohazard."

At 2 A.M. Monday, agents from the Tennessee Bureau of Investigation arrived to process the scene, working until mid-morning to harvest every piece of potential evidence. They found no suspicious fingerprints, no DNA, no forensic evidence at all pointing to the identity of the perpetrator. The bodies were then sent to Memphis for autopsy.

On Thursday, Debbie and Ambria were laid to rest in the Salem Church Cemetery in Gadsden, about fifteen miles southwest of Milan.

Governor Don Sundquist authorized a $2,500 reward per victim for information leading to the apprehension, indictment and conviction of the person or persons responsible for the murder of the 28-year-old woman and her daughter, a second-grader at the school in Medina.

The Gibson County Sheriff's Department, with assistance from both the state investigators and the Federal Bureau of Investigation, considered more than twenty suspects before rejecting them.

BEFORE the bodies were found, Sells was states away. He hired on with a carnival in Greensboro, North Carolina. Soon that job would take him to San Antonio, where a 9-year-old girl would face his rage.

CHAPTER TWENTY-ONE

FIESTA, a ten-day, citywide celebration, erupted on the streets of San Antonio as usual in April 1999. Each one of the 150 events raised money for charitable programs, but for most area residents and tourists, it is simply an excuse for an extended party.

The event was a parade lovers' paradise: three different opportunities to cozy up with masses of spectators, to get vicarious pleasure from the beaming faces of children and to celebrate life with loud music, colorful costumes and waving dignitaries.

Fiesta festivities kicked off one story below street level, down on the Riverwalk. Any place the narrow walkway broadened enough, chairs were placed and tickets were sold. At the Arenson River Theatre, an outdoor facility carved into the bank, spectators squeezed into the long tiers of grass-topped benches cut into the hill. Faces poked out of every window on the upper stories of the buildings lining the San Antonio River. The Texas Cavaliers rode on literal floats that glided down the waterway through a cheering crowd of 225,000.

Midway through Fiesta, the Battle of Flowers Parade high-stepped its way through downtown San Antonio. Floats festooned with flowers and numerous marching high school bands dominated the festivities. They wended their way through the streets, issuing a siren call to one and all. Then, like a platoon of pied pipers, they led the spectators to Alamo Stadium where 3,600 high school band members competed for glory.

The rousing procession that finished the week-and-a-half-long event was the Fiesta Flambeau Parade. Onlookers lined the nighttime streets for the largest illuminated parade in the nation. Torches held aloft, twirling batons with twin flames in their tips and lights in every shape and color bedazzled the crowd. Oohs, ahs and gasps ricocheted through the jostling bodies. And Fiesta came to a dramatic end in an explosion of lights.

But Fiesta is much more than parades; it's a boisterous multi-cultural bash. At the Taste of New Orleans in the Sunken Gardens, taste buds were tantalized with the spicy piquancy of the heaping mounds of red rice and beans, alligator-on-a-stick and other Creole delights—all devoured to the accompaniment of Cajun music. Participants also experienced a little bit of the old country at Fiesta Gartenfest, an oompah-blaring blend of loud polka music, sausage and dark German beer.

The queen of all the events was NIOSA—Night in Old San Antonio—a four-day party in La Villita, the spot of the city's original settlement. Crowds milled through a rabbit warren of narrow, pedestrian-only streets that wove between buildings built of adobe or stone. It was a cascading cacophony of music, intoxicating aromas and shoulder-to-shoulder partiers. Walking through was like twisting a radio dial and hitting a multitude of stations broadcasting everything from mariachi music to an Irish jig, from a rousing polka to a country and western ballad. The 240 food booths kept the mobs moving with unsatisfied hunger to sample one ethnic flavor after another—potato specialties in the Irish section, escargot and champagne from the French, tacos, gorditas and fajitas in the Mexican area and turkey legs and "armadillo eggs" for a taste of Texas. And everywhere you went, there was beer—lots and lots of beer—served in plastic NIOSA souvenir cups. Hardcore revelers balanced a small tower of empties as they made their way to more.

For regal pageantry, there was a decades-old coronation ceremony inducting the Queen and her Duchesses bedecked in their elaborate hand-beaded dresses and heavy, trailing trains. As a counterpoint, laughs abound at the

Corny-nation, a satire that mocked the traditions, politicians and life of San Antonio.

Present at every event, every day, were the *cascarones*, colorful confetti-filled eggs created for revelers to break over one another's heads for good luck and a fun fiesta. Scraps of painted egg shells and bits of paper stuck to the soles of everyone's shoes.

Of course, no big event like this one would be complete without the rides, games of chance and flashing lights of a carnival. Working there in April 1999 was Tommy Lynn Sells.

ONE of the largest free celebrations was Fiesta del Mercado, running daily from late morning until midnight. In downtown's historic Market Square, or El Mercado, six stages featured live entertainment from folkloric dancers to jazz, tejano, conjunto and country and western music. The air was redolent with tempting offerings—spicy Mexican specialties, Cajun shrimp and funnel cakes drenched in mountains of powdered sugar.

On April 18, Mary Bea Perez, an excited 9-year-old, went to El Mercado with her extended family. Like all Fiesta events, this one is heavily patrolled by police officers on foot, on bicycle and mounted on horseback. It was considered a safe, family-friendly venue.

Around 10 o'clock that night, Mary Bea followed her uncle to a booth where he bought a round of beer for the adults in the family. He did not realize that she trailed behind him. When he returned to the group, the tiny third-grader was no longer following.

IN the midst of the swirling sounds of music, the heady aromas of tasty food and an ever-moving crowd of bustling bodies, Sells snatched Mary Bea and spirited her away. He hustled the terrified child into his truck. "We're going to take a little ride," he said. He then forced her down on the floorboard, where she huddled, shivering with fear.

A mile and a half from El Mercado, just west of the

downtown area, they came to a stop near the stockyards. Sells pulled Mary Bea out of his vehicle and through a hole in the fence. In an isolated, trash-strewn spot near a creek, he laid her down on a queen-size mattress. The bedding had already been used many times by illicit couples in search of secret trysts since the day it was dumped there by its original owner. On this soiled surface, Sells forcibly undressed her as she pummeled him with powerless fists, scratching futilely at her attacker with pink-polished fingernails.

When he finished his assault on her body, he wrapped her Mickey Mouse tee shirt around her neck and slowly strangled her to death.

AT El Mercado, her family was frantic. For two hours they searched Market Square for little Mary Bea. Then they walked home, hoping they would find her there, safe and sound. But she was not, and they called the police to report her disappearance.

The whole city was alarmed. This kind of thing just does not happen at Fiesta. A pall settled over the annual celebration. Families with small children thought twice before taking them to any event. Prayers for Mary Bea's safe return flowed from pulpits and households all over town.

In the middle of their pleas, a heavy rain fell. Unnoticed, the child's abandoned body was washed downstream from the place it was discarded.

Ten days after that fateful night in El Mercado, the prayers stopped. A man fishing with his son found the partially clothed, badly decomposed body of Mary Bea Perez in Azalan Creek.

MARY Bea's death was the tragic ending of a sad little life. While living with her mother, Patricia Guerrero, Mary Bea and her little brother, Gabriel, grew up without security, comfort or a sense of being loved. She did not have their father, Alejandro Perez, in her life—he had been shot to death on a sidewalk outside of a tavern when Mary Bea was only two.

The children seldom seemed to be supervised by their mother. They often wandered around the neighborhood hungry. Mary Bea was known to knock on a door, proclaiming that the resident must be a wonderful cook because the meal she was preparing smelled so good. Compassionate women took pity on the two and invited them in for a meal. Other times, they would respond to Mary Bea's pathetic pleas for some food for Joey, her little kitten. Despite the maternal care she witnessed at home, the 9-year-old was very solicitous of her pet and her baby brother.

Everyone heard the loud noises from the frequent conflicts between mother and daughter. From time to time, someone became concerned enough to call in the authorities. Police officers and Child Protective Service caseworkers beat a weary path to their door in the Nob Hill Apartment complex on the northwest side of town. Often, they left with Mary Bea in tow.

At the time of her disappearance and death, Mary Bea was living in the home of her paternal grandmother, Juanita Perez.

A concerned community rallied to form the Mary B warning system. When given word by law enforcement, every radio station in the area broadcasts a bulletin to alert everyone that a child is missing.

The plight of the young girl touched the hearts of three Southside DJs, Juan Sequin, Fernando Perez and Noel Sanchez. They heard that the grandparents were having difficulty paying for Mary Bea's burial.

"We had children of our own. We wanted to help. It could have been our family," Noel Sanchez said. He worked as a DJ at night. During the day, he was the working co-owner of Patriot Express Auto Glass.

"Little kids are our future," said Fred Hernandez, a plumber for the city of San Antonio. "The way I feel for my son made it easy to put myself in Mary Bea's family's shoes. We watched the news and we were touched. And when her body was found, we wanted her to have what she deserved—a quiet place to rest."

In one week's time, Sanchez, Perez and Sequin pulled together a special event at Southway Ford on May 1. In addition to providing space for the barbecue and DJ equipment, the car dealership rounded up bicycles, toys from Toys "R" Us and other items for a raffle.

Sequin was also a caterer, so he was in charge of the food preparation. Perez and Sanchez kept the music rolling out of the sound system all day. The funds they raised paid for Mary Bea's headstone and for the balance due on her cemetery plot. The remaining money raised, about $1,600, was donated to the Heidi Search Center. This non-profit organization has been instrumental in the search efforts for many missing persons. They had coordinated the volunteer task force that attempted to find Mary Bea before her body was discovered in the creek bed.

BY the time Mary Bea's body was found and her family's grieving could begin, Sells had returned his truck to Del Rio and shifted his hunting grounds to Lexington, Kentucky.

CHAPTER TWENTY-TWO

RIDING the rails, Sells traveled to Lexington and signed up at Labor Ready. He lived on the streets for a couple of weeks, occasionally renting a room for a day from a woman who worked at a fast-food chicken restaurant on the next street over from the Labor Ready office. He got day jobs at Excel Building Services and the Lexington recycling center. On May 13, he clocked in at Transylvania University.

THIRTEEN-YEAR-OLD Haley McHone was a troubled young girl. Outside of her home, she was known as a sunny child who had never met a stranger and was always willing to lend a hand. She approached life with a boundless energy. She seemed to get along with everyone, except her immediate family. There, she felt like a cowbird in a cardinal's nest. Her family's authoritarian dynamic was alien to her.

Her incompatibility with her immediate family often left her feeling hurt, isolated and alone. Luckily, she had a refuge nearby. She'd zip up the road to the house where her grandmother, Anna Walker, lived. In fact, Haley wanted to move in with her. Anna told her she could when school was out for the summer.

According to her grandmother, "She rebelled against direct orders, but if you asked her to do something, she would do it."

To make a little spending money, Haley would baby-sit, walk dogs and pull weeds all over her neighborhood near the University of Kentucky. When her grandmother was in the hospital, Haley pedaled miles on her bicycle to visit her. If anything at all was in bloom, she always picked a bouquet of flowers to bring to her grandmother wherever she was.

Haley's real problems at home started, her grandmother said, after her stay at Charter Ridge, an adolescent psychiatric facility. Since then, she had been under the care of a psychiatrist and taking the anti-depressant drug Zoloft. Authorities reported that her stay at the facility was prompted by the emotional damage done by an incident of sexual abuse.

On May 13, she was not in school because she had an appointment with her psychiatrist. First thing in the morning, she went up to her grandmother's house for breakfast. Afterwards, she stopped by her home to play a few video games. Then she mounted her silver-gray mountain bike with Day-Glo orange spray-painted grips and headed for Elizabeth Street Park.

As she rode to the park, she kept a sharp eye out for stray dogs. Haley had become very wary of them since she was bitten nearly a month earlier. She was nearing the end of the series of painful shots she needed to guard against the possibility of rabies.

She propped her bike against the end of a set of swings. She pushed off in the dirt beneath a swing, pumping her legs harder and harder to achieve the greatest height possible. Lost in the sensation of the ride, the cooling breeze racing through her hair, she was unprepared for what happened next.

SELLS' predatory instincts ignited when he saw the girl all alone on the swing. He scanned the park—no one was there. His eyes drifted over to the overgrown, wooded section behind the park. Another opportunity presented itself, and he snatched it up.

He shoved her off the swing. One rough hand slapped over her mouth and held on tight. The other arm squeezed her tightly to his side as she struggled. He dragged her kicking and squirming out of the park and out of sight. He dumped her in the undergrowth and debris. Demanding oral sex, he told her if she did what he said, she would not be hurt. Fearful, she obeyed.

Sells then removed her shirt and, sitting behind her, pulled her to his chest. When he heard the sound of voices coming their way, his hand flew back over her mouth. He gripped her securely, keeping her silent and still until a man and woman strolled by on their walk through the park. Haley did not struggle to escape. She thought she would be safer if she didn't put up a fight. She'd already learned that she could survive unpleasant experiences like this one. She just had to do what she was told and she would be okay.

Once the couple was out of hearing distance, Sells yanked off Haley's remaining clothing, pushed her down into a bed of dried leaves and discarded beer cans and raped her. The cans crushed beneath her naked back. The edges of their rims dug into her skin. She fought to hold in the tears, to hold her emotions in check until he was finished and would leave her alone. But her previous experience had not prepared her for what would happen next.

This molester did not use her and then simply walk away. He snatched her shirt off of the ground and wrapped it around her throat. He twisted it tight, exerting pressure to cut off her supply of air. Her hands clawed at the fabric tourniquet around her neck, trying to loosen its grip. He pulled the shirt tighter. Her ragged little fingernails scraped across the back of his hands, but barely left a mark. She reached up, stretching as far as she could, aiming for his eyes. Before her fingers could reach their target, though, Haley passed out. Her hands fell limp as wilted flowers to the ground. Sells maintained his choke hold on her neck without letting up. He knew it would take a few more minutes before the job was done. Long after the last breath of life whispered out of her body, he released his grip.

He pushed her into an indented contour in the ground and shoveled debris over her with his hands. Brushing the leaves off his clothing and running his fingers through his hair, he emerged from the woods. He jumped on Haley's mountain bike and pedaled his way to the projects. There, he sold her bicycle to a Hispanic man for twenty dollars without a second thought.

IT was time for Haley's appointment with her psychiatrist, but her mother, Reba McHone, could not find her anywhere. Reba went to her mother's house, but Anna had not seen Haley since breakfast. The rest of that day, Reba, Haley's father, Michael, and the three older children in the home scoured the neighborhood in search of the young girl. They roamed the streets until well after dark.

AT 11:52 that night, a Lexington police officer found Sells, passed out and drunk, lying in a heap at the foot of a lamppost. He prodded him awake and arrested him for public intoxication. He was released the next morning. Without picking up his last paycheck, he hopped a freight train and disembarked near the Indiana border. He stole a truck near the tracks and drove off. When it broke down, he broke into a small business office, stole some cash, ripped off another truck and headed north.

FOR ten interminable days, Haley's family and the police department stuck up posters about the missing child in an ever-widening circle from her home. Sightings of Haley were reported, but could never be confirmed. Every one ushered in a swell of hope. Each disappointment laid another brick of despair on their chests.

Then, a dog walking with his owner in Elizabeth Street Park picked up a scent. He pulled his owner into the woods. The poor man did not know what had gotten into his pet. He was normally a well-behaved animal, but no amount of tugging or scolding could keep him from this quest. By the time they reached the source of the dog's concern, the smell was overwhelming. The man rushed home and called police. Haley's body had been found.

Soon, the neighborhood was swirling with red and blue

lights, police on bicycles and on foot. After hearing the tragic news, Anna Walker approached one of the officers and said, "It's a little late to be policing the park, isn't it?"

ONCE the yellow crime-scene tape came down, it was replaced with flower bouquets, potted blooming plants and heartfelt notes as a memorial to the slain child. On the evening of May 27, a crowd of 200 teenagers, neighbors, college students and faculty, family and friends gathered in somber reverence for a candlelight vigil.

Haley's body had been found just a hundred yards from the spot on the railroad tracks where another body was found twenty-one months earlier. Christopher Maier, a 21-year-old University of Kentucky student, was beaten to death and left on the tracks. His girlfriend was raped, beaten, cut across her neck and discarded by his side. But she survived. At the time of Haley's death, that case was still unsolved. Then, in June, the murderer of the student was identified as Angel Maturino Resendiz, the man the media had dubbed "the Railway Killer."

Speculation that Resendiz was also guilty of Haley's murder bubbled through Lexington. The Lexington Police Department pursued that possibility, but found it groundless.

In the coming weeks, the community joined hands to landscape the park, clean up the overgrown woods and erect a fence. They also banded together to form a neighborhood watch—vigilance replacing their previous illusions of safety.

Anna Walker grieved deeply at the loss of her grandchild—the girl she called "the soul of my life." From the day the body was found, she continued to spend a part of each day talking to Haley. In an irony unnoticed at the time, a photo of a distraught Anna in Elizabeth Street Park was published in the *Lexington Herald-Leader* seven weeks after Haley's body was discovered. In it, Anna wore a tee shirt that bore two words: "Tommy Girl."

• • •

BEFORE the body was found, Tommy Lynn Sells was under arrest again. He was picked up this time in Madison, Wisconsin, for being drunk and waving around a box-cutter in a threatening manner. The weapon earned him more than his typical overnight stay in the drunk tank. In custody, he assaulted another inmate at the Dade County jail. He slammed the man's face into a table and ground it into the surface until guards restrained him. Sells had not liked what the man had to say.

By June 10, he had come down from the frenzy that consumed him when he attacked his fellow prisoner. In the aftermath, he swam in the depths of despondency. He gave the jailer a handmade hangman's noose and told him, "I want to kill myself."

Released from the county jail on June 24, he raced home to Del Rio. His arrival was greeted with discord. He could not get his job back at Ram Country. He and Jessica fought so ferociously over one of her girls that law enforcement was called to their home. Lieutenant Larry Pope of the Val Verde Sheriff's Department arrived there with a woman from the Texas Department of Protective Services. The allegation had been made that Tommy had molested Jessica's daughter, Samantha. The social worker made it clear: Jessica and her four children could not stay in the trailer with him.

Jessica took her family to her mother's home. On July 3, Sells drove north—next stop, Oklahoma.

CHAPTER TWENTY-THREE

1998 had been a harrowing year for Susan Wofford and her family in Kingfisher, Oklahoma. Fred and Susan had been living in the rural area, thirty miles northwest of Oklahoma City, for twelve years. Before that, they'd lived in the southern outskirts of the city in the town of Norman, where all three of their children had been born.

Ricky was 17, Michael, 14, and their daughter, Bobbie Lynn, had just turned 13 when their troubles began. A phone call from the hospital heralded a season of tragic events. Ricky had been admitted with severe injuries from an automobile accident. He had been sitting in the back seat of a car driven by a friend. That entire seat flew forward through the windshield on impact. The broken glass ripped Ricky's face to shreds, permanently altering his features.

Ricky had healed enough two months later to go out to a basketball game with his brother, Michael. Their father Fred dropped them off at the high school, then disappeared. For two confusing weeks, Susan wondered and worried. She did not know whether Fred was dead or alive. Her mind toyed with every possible scenario. Then law enforcement located his vehicle on a dead-end street very close to their home. His body was sprawled behind the steering wheel with a gunshot wound to his head. Fred had committed suicide.

Only a month later, Susan's son, Michael, was sitting in the passenger seat of a van as it rolled down the highway. The vehicle went out of control. It rolled over in the median strip, sliding to a stop upside down. The roof was smashed down into the tops of the seats. Michael survived only because he had been thrown clear of the van before it rolled onto its roof. But he had sustained serious injuries—broken ribs, a fractured collarbone and punctured lungs. He was barely able to breathe when paramedics arrived. He was rushed to the hospital in critical condition.

Throughout all this turmoil, Bobbie Lynn was the bright spot in Susan's life. She was a joyful, creative girl who was a straight-A student and the comedian of her class. She played baritone sax and trumpet in the school band and competed on the basketball team.

At home, she loved to read and play with her cats. Like many homes out in the country, they had more felines prowling around than would be considered normal in an urban or suburban setting. But Bobbie Lynn knew every single one of them by name. She was more than willing to play mother to a kitten when its real mother disappeared from the scene—nursing it with a bottle until it was ready for solid food.

After all the misery of 1998, Susan Wofford deserved a break. She was not going to get one in 1999.

IN the spring of that year, Bobbie Lynn hit that difficult stage that all parents dread. As her body underwent its natural metamorphosis, her relationship with her mother transformed as well. Susan was used to her daughter trailing her around the house chattering non-stop about everything in her life and every thought that crossed her mind. To Susan, it seemed as if the change in her daughter happened overnight. She became quiet and wanted to spend more time alone in her room. Socializing with friends became far more important than hanging with her family and her passel of cats.

On July 2, 1999, the 14-year-old told her Mom she was going with friends to Canton Lake in Blaine County for the weekend. Susan gave Bobbie Lynn ten dollars spending money for the trip. She watched as her daughter got into their car. She hated to see her going anywhere in an automobile—last year's accidents were still so vivid in her mind. She knew, though that if she stifled the girl, she would surely lose her. So she held her peace while Bobbie Lynn drove away.

Bobbie Lynn never made it to the lake. As planned beforehand, she left that bunch of friends and embarked on a reckless adventure with a group of kids she knew could not gain her mother's approval. It was just another chapter in the common lying game played by teenagers in families across the country. But for Bobbie Lynn Wofford, it was a fatal deceit.

TOMMY Lynn Sells arrived in Kingfisher that same weekend. While he drove up from Del Rio, he drank heavily and injected cocaine throughout the day and into the night. Despite his altered state of consciousness, Sells remembered the details of this night. And his memory marches to the cadence of the evidence uncovered by investigators. North of Oklahoma City, he drove up Route 81, to the town of Waukomis. There, he abruptly turned around and headed south. In the early hours of July 5, he pulled into the first convenience store he saw, Love's in Kingfisher, to inflate a troublesome leaking tire on his '79 Dodge L'il Red Express and to take a look under the hood. The truck, a wedding present from his bride, was his pride and joy. It was an impressive pick-up, even by Oklahoma standards, sporting the shiny chrome stacks one normally sees only on a semi.

At 4 A.M., after selling some cocaine to an older couple in the parking lot, he spotted a slender young woman about 5'5" with blonde hair and blue eyes and multiple earrings. She was using the phone and complaining bitterly about not being able to reach anyone.

Sells saw his opportunity and approached the seventh-grade student. "Why's a pretty woman such as yourself bitching so much?"

She explained she needed a ride home and could not find one.

Sells replied, "Cool. I'll give you a ride. Hop in my

truck." Sells closed the hood and dropped his tools on the truck floor. Bobbie Lynn settled in the passenger seat. Her relief at going home was tinged by guilt about where she had been. She hoped her mother would never find out.

Sells smiled at the girl and pulled out of the parking lot. "Want some coke? I've got some."

"I don't have any money," Bobbie Lynn stalled.

"You have something worth a lot more than money," he said.

Second thoughts wrapped around Bobbie Lynn's throat like a boa constrictor. "I better not go. Take me back to Love's."

Sells' hand flashed across the seat, back-handing the girl in the face with shocking force. "Shut the fuck up!"

Intimidated by the pain and fear, Bobbie Lynn did not move. She stared straight ahead as her mind raced down avenues of regret. Sells drove northwest of Kingfisher and pulled over on a dark, isolated road, near a creek and cemetery. He pulled off her clothes and forced her to perform oral sex while she whimpered and protested. He fondled her young body, intent on raping her. Before he could penetrate her, Bobbie Lynn's desperation overcame her fear. She slapped and scratched her assailant, then aimed a kick at his genitals. Sells' blood-red rage erupted. He grabbed a ratchet off the floor of the truck and rammed it inside her.

Bobbie Lynn still fought back, jerking open the door of the truck, determined to escape into the night. But Sells had a gun. He shot her in the head and she fell from the truck into the dirt on the side of the lonely road.

Now, it was time to clean up the scene before daybreak revealed his crime. He'd been here before. He knew what he had to do. He grabbed her yellow duffle bag and black purse and threw them as far as he could. In flight, the purse disgorged cosmetics and a public library card. The pair of earrings she wore caught his eye. He plucked them from her earlobes and slid them in his pocket.

He also removed the ratchet—too valuable a tool for a car mechanic to leave behind—pulled her clothing back in place and lifted Bobbie Lynn's lifeless body. At 115 pounds, she was an easy burden. Along the way, he lost her tennis shoes in the undergrowth. He disposed of her body in a less conspicuous spot well off the road. Although disheveled, Bobbie's body was again clad in the green khaki pants and white tank top she'd worn when she met him at Love's.

His rage satisfied, the evidence hidden, he pointed his truck toward Texas and drove off into the first glow of dawn.

AT first, Susan Wofford was angry. Bobbie Lynn had violated her trust by not returning home when she was expected. Initially, the authorities treated the disappearance as a runaway. But the community gathered around Susan, searching for her daughter, passing out fliers and assuring her that everything would turn out okay.

When the police listed her daughter as a missing person, her ire had long ago been set aside, leaving a heavy lump of anxiety in its stead. The waiting game began in earnest. July crawled by. Susan's phone rang frequently with callers informing her that Bobbie Lynn had been seen riding with someone in a pick-up truck, with reports that her body had been found at Canton Lake. They were all mind-numbing calls without any basis in fact.

Susan did anything she could to try to distract herself— she played solitaire till the cards turned limp from overuse. She paced from one end of the house to the other, wearing a visible path in the carpet. She tried to lie down and sleep or relax, but she could never get any rest. Toward the end of the month, Bobbie Lynn was added to the case files of the National Center for Missing and Exploited Children.

Unconfirmed sightings poured into the Kingfisher County Sheriff's Department. Susan's agony continued unabated through August, through September, through October. In November, a witness came forward with a description of the man he'd seen talking to Bobbie Lynn in the parking lot of Love's. With the witness' help, Harvey

Pratt, a forensic artist with Oklahoma's State Bureau of Investigation, drew a sketch of the suspect.

The next day, hunters stumbled across a crushed tube of lipstick and a library card bearing the name "Bobbie Lynn Wofford." They ended their hunting trip with this discovery so they could report what they found to the authorities.

Sheriff Danny Graham arrived on the scene. It was a remote spot where teenagers commonly gathered after dark to drink and party. Bobbie Lynn had never been known to frequent this location.

Graham found a tennis shoe, a yellow duffle bag and a black purse. He kept searching, his dread building. Finally, he uncovered a decomposed body that was not much more than a skeleton held together by stained green khaki pants and a dingy white tank top covered with dried blood. The decomposition was so advanced, it was not possible to be certain at the scene, but the massive trauma to the head indicated that she had died of a gunshot wound.

SUSAN Wofford's phone finally rang. It was not the call she wanted. Once the body was found, girls in Bobbie Lynn's age group were rocked with fear. They would not walk to school anymore—not even two or three blocks. Parents, every bit as anxious as their daughters, provided rides to and from school with a smile.

The community was flooded with high anxiety and mothers and fathers restricted freedoms with impunity. Previously flexible parents now demanded to know exactly where their children were every moment of the day. No longer confident of their children's honesty or safety, they called often to check on their whereabouts.

It was December before DNA tests verified what the sheriff and Susan instinctively knew: the bones belonged to 14-year-old Bobbie Lynn.

The devastated mother stumbled through her grief, planning her daughter's funeral. No one knew how Susan could possibly continue to function after this fourth tragedy.

Local churches were too small to hold the large numbers of people wanting to stand by her side and mourn the death of the teenager. Ultimately, the funeral was held in the school gymnasium and that facility only barely contained the overwhelming crowd.

AFTER receiving a tip, investigators centered their case on Deb's Sports Bar, a Kingfisher tavern. Officers searched the bar, the bar owner's residence and four vehicles. They obtained hair samples, drugs, adult videos and ammunition. They interviewed a man and woman who co-managed the bar, as well as two others. It was all to no avail.

The hair samples gathered did not match Bobbie Lynn's. The ammunition found could not be linked to the shooting. The case remained open.

AFTER the funeral, Susan's waiting began anew. This time, she waited for justice. She often thought about her daughter's angel. Three years before she died, Bobbie Lynn had told her mother about the angel dressed in white that appeared to her in the garden. She showed her mother the exact spot where the apparition always presented itself, but Susan could never see it. As a service manager at a Ford dealership, she was a nuts-and-bolts kind of person, more used to finding answers to practical problems than in exploring otherworldly phenomena. She searched the garden many times for some trick of the light or other optical illusion that could logically explain this unearthly vision. She never found an answer. And she never saw Bobbie Lynn's angel.

TOMMY Lynn Sells returned to Del Rio. After two rounds of interviews, the charge that Sells had molested Jessica's daughter was ruled unfounded. Jessica and her children were able to move back in with Sells. He remained at home for a few months with his family and worked for Amigo Auto Sales.

Bill Hughes, Sells' employer, invited Tommy and Jessica to go to services with him at Grace Community Church. Terry and Crystal Harris and their children were at the services, too, that Sunday.

When Terry Harris needed a new vehicle, he wanted to go to a dealership he could trust. He chose Amigo Auto Sales because a fellow church member owned it. The salesman who assisted him in the purchase of the truck was Tommy Lynn Sells.

One evening, Sells showed up at the Harris home and Terry invited him inside. Crystal took one look at his scruffy hair, his beard and his rampant tattoos and uneasiness swept over her. She chided herself for this un-Christian attitude of judging an individual by his appearance. Curiosity compelled her to join the men in the living room and listen in on the conversation.

Sells admitted that he had been in prison. He also said he had an alcohol problem and that it was tearing his marriage apart. He confessed that he did not know what to do to save his relationship with Jessica. "Terry, you are so lucky. You have such a good family. Your children listen. You have a nice wife. A nice home."

Terry listened and offered what advice he could. While the two talked, the children milled about the house in their typical fashion, crossing the living room from time to time, but never seeming to pay much attention to the adults.

Down the hall in their bedroom, Katy confided to Lori, "I don't like the way that man looks at me."

"You oughta tell Dad," Lori said.

"No. He'll just get mad."

"Then tell Mom, Katy."

"She'll just tell Dad," Katy said with that note of exasperation that an older sister always cultivates to use on the younger siblings.

"You oughta tell them anyway."

"If I tell, Dad will beat him up. Then Dad will be in trouble."

"Oh, yeah," Lori conceded. Lori never repeated this conversation to anyone while Katy was still alive.

As Crystal sat with the men in the living room, she developed a morbid fascination with Sells' tattoos—particularly the one poking out of the neck line of his shirt. In a lull in the conversation she could not resist injecting a question: "I've heard that all those prison tattoos have special meaning. What do yours symbolize?"

He turned toward her. His eyes pinned her to the back of the sofa like a specimen to a mounting board. "Lady," he said, "you don't want to know."

These words, and the expression on his face, still dance an ugly rhythm through Crystal's sleepless nights.

ON December 27, 1999, customs reported that Sells had crossed the border from Mexico into the United States. He had a load of drugs and was making a run north.

CHAPTER TWENTY-FOUR

SELLS confessed to committing this crime, but also claimed an inability to remember details because his mind blacked out. What follows is a thoughtful blend of information and conclusions gathered in interviews with law enforcement personnel and with the family and friends of the victims with what was learned from Tommy Lynn Sells—both his recollections of the night and the facts of the case he ferreted out after the fact.

ROUTE 44 runs through Joplin, Missouri, and across the state line into Oklahoma. Less than ten miles from the boundary, State Route 59 cuts west to the small town of Welch.

Down a long driveway off a country road, less than five miles northwest of Welch, was the modest trailer of Danny and Kathy Freeman. They lived there with their daughter, Ashley. An addition built by Danny had doubled the size of the original mobile home. A rock foundation and a walkway dressed up its appearance. Their home had the convenience of telephone service and electricity, but the Freemans did not have running water and used a wood stove to heat their home.

Christmas 1999 was a somber affair for the family, since it was the first one they had celebrated since the death of their only son, 17-year-old Shane. Earlier that year, in a confrontation with Craig County Deputy David Hayes, Shane had been shot to death.

Ashley turned sixteen on December 29. That night, Jeremy Hurst, Ashley's boyfriend, delivered a birthday present to her and stayed for a short visit. Ashley's best friend, Lauria Bible, was spending the night.

While the four occupants of the trailer slept, a nightmare walked the Freeman property. He dodged between the many animal pens dotted across their land, moving ever closer to their home. When he got inside, finding a weapon was easy. Danny Freeman had hunted since he was a child, and his young daughter Ashley had already bagged a buck. From the more than fourteen firearms in the home, the intruder grabbed a shotgun.

He stalked into Danny and Kathy's bedroom, where they rested on a waterbed. The butt of the shotgun slammed into Danny's collarbone to get his attention. The shooter wanted him awake when he died. Then, the barrel was pointed at his head and the ensuing blast drove Danny's body out of the bed and onto the floor. A second shot to Kathy's head killed her where she lay. A knife flashed out, slicing across her nude abdomen. Her intestines disgorged at her side. The blade moved to Danny and he, too, was eviscerated. An axe slammed down once, twice, three times, severing both his forearms and his lower right leg from his body.

In another bedroom, the first shot awakened Ashley and Lauria with a start. When the second shotgun blast echoed down the hall, Ashley recognized the sound as easily as a baby knows its mother's voice. They huddled together, too afraid to move. They struggled to silence the gasps of fear that burst from their lungs with every breath they took. They strained to hear every sound. They struggled to identify the noises they heard, but could not make sense of them.

In the kitchen, the killer was pouring gasoline in a puddle on the floor in front of the wood stove. He splashed some of the flammable liquid on the front of the heater itself. It was a cold night. The stove had been banked well and was still radiant with heat. Smoke rose from its surface instantly; the flames followed in seconds.

Just as the two girls smelled the first faint whiffs of the fire, a figure with the eyes of a madman loomed in the doorway. He lunged toward them. His hands clutched a shotgun aimed at their heads. He ordered them out of the room and into the chilly night. Shoving, hitting, cursing, he herded them into his van. They took off in the darkness before the dawn.

Barreling southwest down Route 44, and then south on Interstate 35, the abductor tormented the two terrified girls and then ended their lives. Sells claimed that somewhere near the Red River, the border between Oklahoma and Texas, he brought the van to a stop and dumped the two teenagers in an isolated area before resuming south. Their bodies have never been found.

A neighbor on the way to work at 6:30 on the morning of December 30 noticed the fire at the Freemans' trailer and called 9-1-1. The Welch Volunteer Fire Department raced to the scene, but the home was a total loss. The only portion of the home intact was the floor of the master bedroom. There, the ruptured waterbed had doused some of the flames.

When the home was searched, only one body was found, the charred remains of 37-year-old Kathy Freeman. Kathy was lying on the carcass of her waterbed. In addition to the absence of bodies, two other items appeared to be missing. Danny had a collection of arrowheads and rudimentary Indian tools that he had gathered since he was a child. His most rare pieces were framed in glass-covered boxes, some hanging on the wall, others stacked in anticipation of finding a spot to be displayed. The more common ones were stored in plastic buckets. Of the thousands of artifacts in Danny's collection, only a handful of splintered shards were ever found.

The second item never recovered was Ashley's savings. She had been working at Roscoes convenience store and squirreling away every penny she could. She had at least $1,100 and possibly as much as $4,000. That cash was wrapped in foil, sealed in a Tupperware container and tucked away in the deep freeze among packages of frozen meat. Ashley's nest egg was never found, but Lauria's purse with her $200 of Christmas money was recovered at the scene.

All day, family and neighbors searched every inch of the Freemans' forty-acre lot on foot and again on horseback. No signs of Danny, Ashley or Lauria were found.

At 5:30 that afternoon, the Oklahoma State Bureau of Investigation, convinced there were no more bodies, released the scene to Danny's half-brother, Dwayne Vancil. At that time, the prevailing theory was that Danny had murdered his wife, torched his home and abducted the two girls. There was one inexplicable detail, though, casting doubt on this conclusion. All of the Freemans' vehicles and Lauria Bible's car were still sitting in the driveway of the Freeman home.

Early the next morning, Lauria's parents, Lorene and Jay Bible, not satisfied with the search of the house, were determined to find some clue to the whereabouts of their daughter. Trudging through the ashes and rubble, it only took five minutes for them to make a startling discovery. Sissy, Ashley's rottweiler, lay on the blackened floor next to the waterbed. When she stood to greet the Bibles, it appeared that she had been lying on the shattered remains of Danny's head. When Lorene pulled back the carpet by that spot, they clearly saw the outline of a second body.

When the sheriff's department and OSBI returned to the scene, they ordered Jay and Lorene off the premises so that they could resume their search. The Bibles refused to leave until the investigators had sifted through every small piece of debris.

Danny Freeman was taken off the list of suspects. Investigators entertained the possibility that Ashley and Lauria were the perpetrators. To the families, it did not quite add up. Lauria's car was out front and her purse with her money and her identification was found in the rubble. Interviews with those who knew the girls, and a search into their backgrounds further diminished the probability of their involvement.

Speculation then centered on three different fronts. The relatives of the Freemans were certain that the crime was connected to Shane's death and Danny's threatened civil suit against the Craig County Sheriff's Department. Even after Deputy David Hayes and his brother, Undersheriff Mark Hayes, passed polygraph tests, the family's suspicions were still firmly entrenched.

Lorene and Jay believed the tragedy was somehow tied to drug trafficking. Although Danny was known to have smoked marijuana and suspected of growing some for his personal use, he'd had no record of drug offenses, and law enforcement had no evidence that he'd sold drugs.

Investigators then set their sights on Steven Ray Thacker, a known killer who was on the run. He was apprehended in early January and put on death row in Tennessee for a stabbing death in Dyersburg. He was also charged with other murders in Oklahoma and Missouri. They could not connect Thacker to the carnage in Welch.

OSBI investigated thirty leads in the murders of Danny and Kathy Freeman and abductions of Lauria Bible and Ashley Freeman. None of the leads solved the case.

The gravesite of 9-year-old Mary Bea Perez, who was abducted from a San Antonio street festival on April 18, 1999, then murdered. Confusion about the time of her death resulted in the wrong date appearing on her headstone. (Diane Fanning)

Snapshots from an ordinary life: Tommy Lynn Sells as a boy in the home of his aunt, Bonnie. His life took a dramatic turn for the worse after he returned to his mother's house. (Courtesy Tommy Lynn Sells)

An adult Sells and his wife, Jessica Levrie, at their October 22, 1998 wedding. (Courtesy Tommy Lynn Sells)

Bags of food and clothing that Fabienne Witherspoon said she had put together for Sells after he had come to her Charleston, WV, home claiming his destitute family needed help. There was no family, and Sells' intentions were far more sinister . . . (Charleston Police Department)

Witherspoon said he attacked her in her bedroom, binding her with strips torn from sheets. (Charleston Police Department)

A close-up on half of the piano stool that Witherspoon said Sells smashed over her head. (Charleston Police Department)

Witherspoon fought back. She said she hit Sells' head with a ceramic duck before making her escape. (Charleston Police Department)

The Harris home, where Krystal Surles was attacked, as viewed from the Betz home, where the 9-year old went in search of help after Sells murdered her best friend. (Diane Fanning)

Though Surles' throat had been slashed, she was able to describe her attacker to police artist Shirley Timmons. (Texas Rangers) Timmons' sketch quickly led authorities to Tommy Lynn Sells, seen here standing in front of his mother-in-law's flood-ravaged Del Rio home in 1998. (Courtesy Tommy Lynn Sells)

Tommy Lynn Sells' artwork

Names are written on the cherries: Bobbie Lynn, Stephanie, and Haley. (Courtesy Tommy Lynn Sells)

"Hillbilly Justice." The name Dardeen is written very small on the axe's blade and may refer to a family that Sells allegedly murdered. One victim died from gunshot wounds; the other three had been bludgeoned to death. (Courtesy Tommy Lynn Sells)

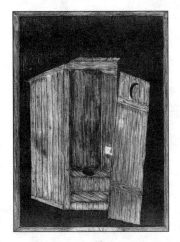

An outhouse. (Courtesy Tommy Lynn Sells)

An optimistic note written by Sells during his trial. (Courtesy Tommy Lynn Sells)

He didn't walk. Polunsky Unit housing, Death Row, Texas, where Sells now lives. (Diane Fanning)

CHAPTER TWENTY-FIVE

WHEN Sells returned home, he faced the wrath of an irate Jessica the second he pulled open the door. He had been gone with her van for days. He'd missed work, and money was needed for household necessities. They drove to the Pico Convenience Store, where Sells tried to get in contact with Bill Hughes on the pay phone to arrange to pick up his last paycheck. He went into the store for a pack of smokes and ran into Terry Harris. The two men talked for about five minutes. Back home, a fight ensued, and Sells left to escape Jessica's anger.

He took refuge at Larry's Lakefront Tavern. There he drank Jim Beam and Coke and chatted up the barmaid, Noel Houchin. According to Noel, Sells was a major nuisance that night. He asked her for sex. He asked her where she lived. He asked her for sex again. When she mentioned that her car was broken down, he offered to pay to have it fixed if she would have sex with him. Finally, he told her that he owned Amigo Auto Sales and she could have any vehicle on the lot if she'd have sex with him.

According to Sells, he did tell her that he worked at Amigo Auto. He also said he was not interested in her himself, but told her that the owner, Bill Hughes, was a "horny old son-of-a-bitch. If she batted her eyes right, he would help her."

At one point in the evening, Sells took a break from drinking and left the bar to change from the shorts he was wearing to a pair of pants. When he emptied the pockets of his shorts, he realized he must have grabbed someone else's money, too, when he scooped up his change.

He returned to the tavern and discovered that the money belonged to Sonny, a friend and neighbor of his at American Campgrounds. He turned it over and sat down for another Jim Beam and Coke. He was one of the last two patrons to leave the bar after it closed at 2 A.M..

Sells stopped on his way home near the flea market, where an older woman had an outside refrigerator. He reached inside and pulled out some venison and a beer. While he ate, he decided he'd go down to Terry Harris' house and get the money he claimed was owed to him. Sells insisted, after his arrest, that he had fronted cocaine to Terry Harris in exchange for a promised $5,000. No corroborating evidence has surfaced to support this allegation.

He left the property when the woman's son, visiting his mother for the holidays, pulled up to the house. Sells stopped by his trailer and picked up one of his long-bladed knives that sat outside. Jessica was never aware of his presence.

SELLS drove Jessica's van east on Route 90 toward Del Rio. Just before he reached Lake Amistad, he turned left and drove through the stone arch to Guajia Bay. After curving left and right, the road dipped down before heading up to the homes on the hill. Sells parked the van at the lowest point and went the rest of the way on foot.

He approached the house as quietly as any four-legged predator on the prowl, but it was not noiseless enough for the Harrises' dog. Sells had to pause and pet him before he could break into the trailer and murder Katy Harris and slice the throat of Krystal Surles.

Down the hall, a noise woke up Justin. He didn't know what he had heard but, unconcerned, he got up and went to the bathroom. Sells emerged in the living room and headed for the back door. Justin's alarm had been set to help him avoid wetting the bed. It chose that moment to blare out its obnoxious wake-up signal. Sells slipped down the hall, shut off the alarm and then left the trailer by the back door. Justin returned to his room, still unaware of the intruder's presence. He assumed one of his sisters had cut off the alarm and he went back to sleep.

Sells took his bloody knife with him when he left the house. He stopped outside to snatch up the two screens he'd removed from the windows earlier and drove farther down Route 90 to the lake. On the bridge, he threw the screens as far as he could and listened until they splashed in the water.

At home, he washed the blood off of his hands, undressed and crawled into his king-size waterbed. He pleaded with Jessica to hold him. She wrapped her arms around his body and clutched him tight until he drifted off to sleep.

He awoke at noon and Jessica was already up and gone. He arranged for the sale of his truck, but would have to wait until Monday when the credit union opened to get the money. He decided there was one more thing to do before he left town. He had to get back at Frances Cuzak, an attorney and federal public defender who had ticked him off. A short time before, he had met her son at a bar and gone with him to Frances' home. He'd monopolized the telephone all evening until she'd told him she had calls to make. Her attitude deeply offended Sells. He planned to kill her on Sunday night.

His future settled, he walked up to the house of the friend he'd run into at the bar the night before. They drank whiskey and beer and shot up cocaine. He staggered home from Sonny's at one point, but an angry Jessica threw his clean clothes out in the yard and told him not to come back until he sobered up. She slammed the door in his face and locked it. Sells returned to Sonny's house.

AFTER Sells was inside Sonny's place, the sheriff set up surveillance of the trailer where Sells lived. Not wanting to make him aware of their presence before they had a warrant, they stayed on the other side of the street. Ironically, Sells was not in his home, but at Sonny's, on the same side of the street where the officer had set up to watch him.

Sells got busy working the phone. He made several threatening calls to his mother-in-law, Virginia Blanco. She reported these messages to the sheriff's department. When asked by deputies if they should move in and take Sells now, Pope said, "Put the mother-in-law in a motel. Don't park her car there, just put her in a motel. Make sure her car's nowhere near that motel. Then she's safe, forget it and just keep watching that trailer."

Many hours later, he did return. Although he was still under the influence of drugs and alcohol, Jessica unlocked the door and let him in.

A deputy placed an urgent call to Pope soon after Sells' arrival home. "Somebody screamed in the trailer, we want to go in."

"No, no, don't. Did you hear one scream?"

"Just one."

"Well, one of two things happened. Somebody stubbed their toe and yelled, or somebody cut somebody's throat, in which case you're too late. You hear any more screams, then you can get in there. Just watch it—watch the trailer."

Unaware of the concern outside, Sells went to bed and slept until the authorities arrived with an arrest warrant for capital murder.

CHAPTER TWENTY-SIX

AFTER Sells was booked at the Val Verde Correctional Center, he sat down with Lieutenant Larry Pope and Texas Ranger Johnny Allen while the video camera rolled. Sells' tough-guy demeanor softened considerably once that little red light went on.

Pope stated that the date and time was January 2, 2000, at 8:06:46 A.M.. "Okay, let's introduce ourselves around here. I'm Larry Pope, Lieutenant with the Val Verde Sheriff's Department, Criminal Investigations Division."

"My name is Allen, John Allen with the Texas Rangers, stationed here in Del Rio."

"And I'm Tommy Sells. They put me under arrest for a murder we just talked about."

"You've been read your rights once tonight already and I want to take this opportunity to read them to you again," Pope began.

"I understand that, and I waived all my rights," Sells said.

"Well, let me read them to you," Pope said and continued on with the standard recitation.

Sells seemed distracted, fiddling with the watchband on his arm.

Pope warned him, "If there's something you don't want to talk about, you should not lie about it. You should just say, 'I don't want to talk about it.' It's your right. Now I advise you, if you lie about it, if it came out, it would just make you look bad."

"I understand."

The preliminaries finished, the questioning and official

recorded confession began. "Tommy, you were arrested for the murder of . . ." Pope said.

"I don't know," Sells interrupted.

"You don't know her first name? You know her nickname—what they call her by? You don't know who she is? You know she's the Harris girl?"

"Yeah."

"Terry Harris' first girl?" Pope clarified.

"Right."

"We know her as Kathleen or Kathy . . ." Pope began.

"Kaylene," Allen corrected.

"Kaylene, excuse me, or Katy, and there was another girl there also. You were also arrested for attempted murder on her. Do you know that girl's name or anything?"

"No."

Pope and Allen established the identity of the second girl as Krystal Surles and confirmed that Sells agreed to talk about what happened.

Sells said, "I was going to do a lawyer today. I was wanting to kill a lawyer."

"What lawyer?" Allen asked.

"Lives across the street."

"From the campgrounds?"

"Yeah, across the street from the campgrounds."

"What for?" Allen queried.

"Well, I guess . . ."

Pope interrupted, "When were you going to kill him?"

"Her," Sells clarified.

"Her."

"Just . . . How can I explain this to make any sense? She stepped over my foot somewhere and I didn't like it. I was going to get revenge on her."

After a break to light cigarettes and adjust the volume control on the microphone, Pope continued, "The point we agreed to start on, I believe, was the evening of December 30, 1999, when you meet in Del Rio some place with Terry Harris."

"Uh, okay."

"Tell me, who-all was there and where did you meet?"

"We met at Pico's station—I think it's Pico's, it's . . ."

Allen interjected, "It might be Shamrock or something?"

"It's right by Ram Country. Me and my wife were in there, I was buying a pack of cigarettes. Terry pulls up. Me and Terry went inside. I stopped to make a phone call, that's the reason I was there. Uh, me and Terry goes inside for a little while—less than five minutes—We talked for less than five minutes. We came back out and he told me he was going to Kansas. I asked him when he was going to pay me my money. He said his buddy had hit a deer with his car and he was going up to Kansas to get his truck or something."

"Did he owe you money?" Allen asked.

"Yeah."

"Well, how much money did he owe you?"

"Less than five thousand dollars," Sells said.

"Why would he have owed you that?"

"Cocaine," he said.

"Coke?" Pope asked.

"Yeah, I guess coke fronted to me and I fronted to him. He never made payments since then."

"This is all five thousand dollars' worth of cocaine at one time or over a period of time, how did that accumulate?"

"No, it was just one time."

"One time?" Allen asked. "You gave him five thousand dollars' worth at one time?"

"Actually, I owed three thousand dollars on it and I charged him five."

"Okay."

"I had to make some money for me."

"Yeah, I understand business," Allen responded. "How long ago?"

"Oh, uh, two months ago."

"Two months ago?"

"Yeah, give or take." Sells shrugged his shoulders and

leaned forward, resting his elbows on his knees.

"All right. And he didn't—did he or didn't he—pay you that night?" Pope asked.

"No."

"Okay. And what was your general consensus? What did you think? Was he handling it? Was he going to pay you something, or what? What was your opinion?"

Sells shook his head. "It didn't strike me then. It didn't strike me."

"Well, did it upset you or anything?"

"I didn't give it much thought."

"Okay," Pope conceded.

"To tell you the truth, I don't remember. I said, 'I'll see you later.'"

"Okay."

"And me and the wife went on and once there, we got into an argument and I went to the bar and got drunker than hell. And when I left the bar, I started, I stopped down at that there flea market a little up above the campgrounds."

Pope shook his head, "Yes. The one down in that hole."

"Yeah, yeah."

"Where the road goes way down?"

"I stopped down there and ate some deer meat or something they had in the refrigerator back there. And then, it was just like a bell went off in my head. It's just like it said, 'That's what you can do.'"

"Meaning what?" Allen asked. "What do you mean when you said, 'That's what I can do'?"

"Go down to Terry's place. I didn't go down there to kill. I didn't go down there to rape. I didn't go down there—I just say—go down there. It wasn't premeditated, you know. It's like that girl in Kentucky, you know. I didn't premeditate it. It just happened. And I went through the window where the little blind boy used to sleep. He said . . ."

Pope broke in, "Let's back up first. You talked a little earlier about, uh, the weapon that you chose to take."

"Well, it wasn't chosen. It was what I had with me."

"When you left your house—Did you take anything with you when you left your house?" Allen asked.

"Yeah, the knife."

"And, it was . . ."

Sells held up his hands to demonstrate the length of the knife. "About that long."

"Handle and blade and all?"

"Yeah."

"Okay," Allen said. "A little bit over twelve inches. What kind of blade did it have on it?"

"A thin one, long one, with a little tip."

"So you eat deer meat and say, 'That's what I can do.' So, where'd you go? What happened?"

"Well, I go down to Terry's house. I fuck around with the dog a little bit outside, then I figure out how to get in the trailer. I'm so drunk," Sells said with a smile, "I'm surprised I didn't wake up half of Del Rio, I'm so drunk. It's like a blur. I finally figured out a way to get in the trailer."

"How did you get in?" Allen asked.

"I tried to jimmy the back door at first. I tried to get into the back door to begin with and I was too drunk. I screwed that up." Sells' body language relaxed. His tone of voice became jocular. It was as if he were describing a high school prank. "I couldn't get in there. And then I tried a window by the living room by the back side of the trailer. Couldn't get in and actually I was walking around to leave and I noticed a window up. That's by where the water tank was."

"On the back? Front? What?" The edginess in Allen's voice reflected his discomfort.

"The front." Sells reacted to Allen's tone and straightened in his seat.

"I wondered, did you know whose window it was?"

"I didn't at the time. When I got in, I did. It was the little blind one."

"It was whose room?" Allen asked again.

"Their little boy—the blind little boy."

"Okay. That's where the water tank is?"

"Yeah."

"How did you get through that window?"

"It was open. I took the screen off, but the window was open."

"Okay."

"I climbed in and went to . . ."

Allen interrupted, "When you climbed in, did the little boy say anything?"

"Yeah. Yeah. I woke him up when I climbed in. He said, 'I wish you all would stop coming in my room,' and I walked on out of the room and stood."

"By that, you think he thought it was maybe his sisters in there?"

"Yeah."

"You don't think he thought it was you."

"No," Sells shook his head.

"Okay, you walk out of that room and where do you go?"

"Into the dining room. There's the dining room, the kitchen and the front room. I stood in that room for a few minutes and said, 'What the hell am I doing?' And now, it's like, at the point where you're all pumped up, you know? It's bad circumstances. I thought about doing them all."

He described his exploration of the bedrooms as he nervously played with his fingers. "I know it seems kind of bizarre that there's no plan-out. It was on the spur." He said that then he thought about raping the mother, but was too drunk to act upon it.

When his description reached Kaylene's bedroom, Pope asked, "First time you cut her or you stabbed her . . . ?"

"I stabbed her, in the arm, I think. She started to say something and I poked the knife at her and I said, 'Shut up.' And she made some kind of comment like, 'You didn't have to cut me.' And I said, 'Shut the hell up.' And she told that little girl to go get her mom."

"Does that little girl know you?" Allen asked. "Has she ever seen you before?"

"Yeah, yeah, not the one on the top bunk, I don't think."

"But the one standing by the bed?"

"Yes."

"Okay," Allen responded.

"And, I, uh, cut her to shut her up," Sells added.

"Where did you cut her the next time?" Pope asked.

"In the stomach," Sells tossed off as casually as someone else would state the dressing preference for his salad.

"With a lot of force?"

"That damn knife was so sharp, it just didn't take a lot of force. No, sir. I heard somebody say that I cut her fingers and shit off, but if I did, I didn't mean to do that. I just slit her throat."

"Well, there's an awful lot of rumors going on about everything," Allen explained. "Now you said you cut her throat. Was she facing you? Was she away from you? Can you remember anything? If you're not sure about something, you're not sure. I understand that—a lot of things went fast."

"I just reached out and went *psssht*." His face was devoid of every emotion but boredom. "That's how sharp that knife was."

"Which hand would you have had the knife in?" Allen asked.

"I believe it was this one," he said wriggling the appropriate wrist.

"The right hand?"

"Yes."

"She's in front of you?"

"Uh-hunh. As me and you are looking at each other. I took the knife and it was dealt with. And she fell down and I . . ."

"Stuck her?" Pope interjected.

"No. Cut her some more again till I was sure it was all the way—It was a done deal."

"Was there much fighting in the area?"

"Nah."

"Not really? All right. Okay. As long as that's the best you remember."

"And the little girl in the top bunk was petrified. And I done dropped the first one and I started to walk out of the room. Then, I walked back over to the top bunk and I just *psssht*," he said, making a slicing motion with his hand. "And I thought I killed her."

"She's in the top bunk, did you reach up, jump up or crawl up on the bed?"

"No, it was simple. I just reached over."

"How was she laying down? How was she in the bed?" Allen asked.

"I believe she was on her back."

"Just not moving—petrified?"

"Yeah."

"Was she saying anything?" Allen continued.

"Not a word. She didn't scream. She didn't do nothing, nothing," he answered. "I'm sorry for giving you all so much hassle."

The officers assured him that they were just doing their job. They then proceeded to question him about what happened after he left Kaylene's room.

"I walked out of the room. I go to the back door," he said.

"Did you close the door or leave the door open?" Pope asked.

"I don't know."

"Still had the knife in your hand?"

"Yeah," he said. Then he added, "I still got the knife. Well, in a roundabout way, I know where it's at. I don't know why I didn't throw that into the lake. But when I left, I just walked through the house and I think I went back to her mom's room for a brief moment. And I was, like, 'Just get out of here,' you know? I think I was getting panicky. And then I just walked out the back door."

"You said, 'I don't know why I didn't throw that knife in the lake,'" Allen said. "Did you throw something else in the lake?"

"When I went out the back door, I know I took the screens off. The back one, I grabbed it and walked back around to the front. I, like, don't think you found any of my prints out there, you might've, but I doubt it. I was pretty careful about that."

"Were you careful about not touching something, or did you wipe them off?"

"Wipe them off."

After Pope and Allen elicited all the details they could about the disposal of the screens, Allen asked, "You said you were in the van?"

"Yeah."

"Which van is that?"

In response, Sells' face expressed the first sign of genuine concern during the confession. "My wife's van. It's all she's got. Please don't take it from her."

"Back up a minute, Tommy," Allen said. "What reason would there have been to cut that girl's underwear?"

"Just to make it look like that."

"Look like what?"

"Like a rape scene or something, I don't know, like . . ."

Allen interrupted. "Was there ever any attempt at any kind of sexual assault?"

"No," Sells insisted. "I didn't touch her or nothing. I'm telling you I done it right? That's the way it happened. I didn't try to screw her or nothing. I didn't."

"It's like I told you," Pope said. "All I want is the truth. If you get some part of it you don't want to answer, just say, 'I don't want to answer that.'"

"I'll tell you, I don't mind. I'm glad it's over with."

"Why are you glad it's over with?" Allen asked.

"Hurting people ain't good."

"Do you think, Tommy, you would have continued?"

"I know without a doubt, I wouldn't have stopped."

CHAPTER TWENTY-SEVEN

EARLY in the afternoon of January 2, Pope, Allen and Sells went out to the Harris home to videotape a walk-through of the crime scene. Allen operated the camera. Pope did the questioning. They started down at the spot where Sells had parked the van that night. They walked up the path he'd followed to the trailer. Sells circled the home, showing them the door he'd attempted to jimmy, the window he'd tried to open and where he'd actually entered the home.

He crawled back in through that window again and casually revisited the site of the carnage. He re-enacted all his movements through the home and into Kaylene's bedroom. "She tried to come over here." He stood in the spot by the bedroom door. "And I stabbed her like right here somewhere."

He moved to the end of the bunk bed and said, "I stabbed her here and she, like, jumped back, and I cut her like this right here." He nonchalantly demonstrated the flick of a knife blade across the girl's throat. "She fell down right here," he said as he bent down to the floor, "and I think I reached down there and done it one more time."

He walked over to the side of the top bunk. "And this little girl up here, and I walked over her and went like this." His hand made a puny flip of the wrist over the spot where Krystal's neck had lain that night.

"This girl just fell down? There was no more struggle or anything?" Pope asked. "'Cause I'm looking at this room and I see blood over here, here, here." As he pointed out the blood, Allen scanned the area with the camera. "Is there any more movement than that?" Pope continued,

"Now, I know you may not remember everything but do you know how some of this blood may have gotten around this room?"

"Maybe when the little girl got up. Right here"—he moved to the foot of the bunk bed and pointed to the floor—"was the main conflict. And I walked over here"—he returned to the side of the bed—"and I cut this one. Then I was getting a little nervous."

Before returning to the Val Verde Correctional Center, the officers and Sells stopped by Val Verde Regional Medical Center and drew up blood samples for forensic testing.

Lieutenant Pope had videotaped a confession and a walk-through of the crime scene. The district attorney wanted more—he requested a written confession, too.

In that session with Sells, Pope asked, "Tommy, did you take a souvenir or something?"

"No, I don't ever take anything," Sells answered.

With that denial, there was no evidence of felony theft, since the family could not identify any items missing from their home except for the two window screens.

Pope typed up the confession with a standard phrase establishing Sells' identity and a list of his constitutional rights. Sells initialed each of the rights and signed each page. One statement was made in this confession that differed from his videotaped accounts. Sells said, "I touched her between the legs and I touched her breast."

The comment did not resonate then with the sleep-deprived investigator. The next morning, however, Pope could not shake it out of his mind.

He had the prisoner brought from his cell to Pope's office and said to him, "Look, in the State of Texas, when you're under arrest, anything you tell me can't be used in court unless you write it down and sign it, or it's recorded somehow or another. So I want to ask you something. What did you mean when you said you touched her between the legs? Did you rub her? Did you put your fingers inside her? What did you do?"

"I put my finger inside her," Sells admitted.

"Now, I'm going to tell you something. In the State of Texas, that is rape. With a rape and a killing, that's a capital punishment. That means you get the death sentence."

Sells looked at Pope, but said nothing.

"What I want you to do is give me a statement that says that, but I told you what it can do."

"Well, it's the truth."

"Okay. I'll take it."

Pope prepared and Sells signed the following statement on January 7, 2000, at 5:04 P.M..

Last night, I gave Inv. Pope a written statement. In that statement, I told him I touched the Harris girl between her legs before I cut her with the knife I had.

Today Inv. Pope called me into his office and told me he wanted to know more details about this touching, if I was willing to tell him. He wanted to know if I rubbed her between the legs or patted her or if I put my finger in her vagina. I told him I put my finger in her vagina. He then told me he could not repeat what I told him in court.

He then asks me if I was willing to put it in writing and sign it. He said if I did that it could be used in court and the fact that I had put my finger in her vagina against her will, would be a rape and this would result in me being charged in CAPITAL MURDER and this would probably result in me be [sic] sentenced to DEATH.

I told him it was the truth and I was willing to give a written statement. When I went into the bedroom where the murder happened, I got in the bottom bunk bed with the Harris girl. I don't know her first name but I knew she was kin to Terry Harris. I don't know what I said but I threatened her with the knife to keep her quiet. I cut her panties off and I cut or pulled her bra off. I touched her breast and I put my hand between her legs and

I put my finger in her vagina. Shortly after that she jumped out of bed and I have told the rest.

I know this statement can result in me getting the death penalty. I don't want to die but it's the truth and I just don't want to hurt anyone else.

I am giving this statement of my own free will and it is true and correct to the best of my ability. I fully realize that I do not have to give any statement or talk to anyone and if I want to talk to anyone I can have an attorney present before I talk. I do not want an attorney present and I have not requested an attorney at any time since my arrest.

And the confessions didn't stop. One murder after another tripped off his tongue. Haley McHone, May 1999. When asked why he'd killed her, he said, "She was in the wrong place at the wrong time." The Dardeen family, November 1987. When describing Eileen, he said, "She was big in the front." For some reason, he was uncomfortable saying that she was pregnant. Ena Cordt, July 1985. A forged document surfaced and rumors swirled that a judge had paid for her murder because he was having an affair with her and she was causing trouble. Mary Bea Perez, April 1999. He sat on the floor of the rest room and demonstrated how he'd strangled her.

The list went on and on. Some provided no easy means of verification. In St. Louis, for example, Sells claimed that when he worked for Atlas Towing in 1986, he'd received a call from a 25- to 30-year-old prostitute whose car had broken down. When he got to her disabled vehicle, she did not have any money. Sells suggested a trade: she would have sex with him and he would take care of her car. When she wasn't interested in the deal, he shot her and threw her body in the river.

Pope and Sells had frequent conversations outside of official interrogations during his time in the Val Verde Correction Center, which housed the jail as well as all the offices of the sheriff's department.

In one talk, Pope asked, "Tommy, I can see how you kill these girls. You're stronger than them and stuff. But how do you kill those men and not get roughed up in the process?"

Sells was on his feet before Pope's lips had a chance to close. His hand flashed out and drew a line across the lieutenant's throat. "Once you cut their throat," he said, "their hands are at their throat and you've got no hands to worry about."

Sherrif D'Wayne Jernigan played a role in keeping the confessions flowing. He spent hours in the cell with his prisoner talking to him about his spiritual well-being. Another prisoner, Jose Cerveray, gave Sells a Bible that he just tossed on the floor. Jernigan picked the book up and encouraged him to read Isaiah 55:7. "Let the wicked forsake his way, and let the unrighteous man his thoughts: and let him return unto the Lord, and he will have mercy upon him; and to our God, for he will abundantly pardon."

The sheriff returned to the cell regularly, often bringing a tin of snuff. He always greeted the prisoner with a handshake and a hug. When Cerveray was shipped off to prison, he gave Sells a plant he had raised in his quarters. The sheriff's wife brought in a second plant to adorn Sells' room.

Eventually, the religious exhortations of the sheriff, the neighboring inmate, his wife and his mother-in-law led Sells to believe he had found the Lord. In an outdoor, enclosed compound, a prison minister baptized him in a large tub.

As soon as Terry Harris could arrange for Kaylene's body to be shipped to Kansas, the rest of the family followed. They lived with Crystal's mother for most of January. Crystal and Terry knew they had to get the kids back in school. They left the warm embrace of family with great reluctance and moved back to their home near Del Rio at the end of the month.

It was impossible to sleep in their old home. Every little bump or whisper in the night spiked the level of adrenaline in their bloodstreams. During the day, every room echoed with Katy's presence.

At work, Terry found that his ability to concentrate was impaired and the responsibilities of a familiar job were now overwhelming. One afternoon, two weeks after their return, Terry called Crystal from his office. "I want to go home."

"Come home. We'll pack everything up and just go."

Crystal had understood without a word of explanation. They moved back to Kansas on Terry's birthday, February 12.

WHEN the body count from his confessions reached fifty, Sells claimed that he was only 70 percent finished.

In the midst of all these confessions, Ranger Smith's curiosity was piqued by Sells' lifestyle. "Tommy, you go off on all these little adventures, you gotta eat. If you don't want to eat, you gotta buy your dope. They're not gonna give it to you. You ain't gonna work. How do you make any money?"

"Well, I can make three to five hundred dollars a day holding a sign that says, 'Homeless. Please help. God Bless.' I can make even more with a woman and a child with me," Sells said. He expanded on this scam later in a letter. "I was thinking about some of the ways I made money as a homeless person. Was it a con? I don't believe so. 'Homeless will work for food. Please Help.' Or be at spring break on some beach, Daytona's one of the best, have a one-step camera, point, push the button. Or wash windows." He added that homelessness was not a lifestyle he was forced to live. It was one he preferred.

"Almost anyplace you put up that sign, you can get a fast 20 or so, you do it when the traffic is the heaviest, between lights. The same with the windows just steal a squeegee. And the camera thing is always good in a place: beach, riverwalk."

•   •   •

CALLS started coming in to the Texas Rangers from California to New England. After the calls, many came to talk to Sells in person about their cases. They listened to him with hope, relief and horror as he recounted details. Thirteen murders were confirmed in a short time.

Not all seekers of justice found answers from Tommy Lynn Sells. On November 18, 1993, 9-year-old Angie Housman had been abducted from her home in O'Fallon, Missouri, near St. Louis. Her assailant had raped and tortured her, leaving her bound to a tree, where she died of exposure. An unidentified black teenaged girl was found in a boxcar on April 2, 1996. She was wrapped in sheets in the train when it stopped at the Tropicana Plant near Bradenton in Manatee County, Florida. She died of suffocation. But their tormentor was not Tommy Lynn Sells. At the time of both these crimes, he was a guest of the penal system in West Virginia.

Sells told his questioners that he had a dream about the murders of Pamela Casteneda and her mother, Margaret McClain. The crime occurred in Charleston, West Virginia, on September 7, 1991. At first, it was considered a possibility that Sells was making an indirect confession with some wiggle room. The prosecution team in Del Rio nurtured this suspicion for quite some time. In fact, District Attorney Thomas Lee cited it in a response to the defendant's pre-trial motion in July. It was one of the murders he listed as evidence of extraneous crime or bad acts. Nonetheless, another man, Dana December Smith, is still behind bars for this crime. His DNA was a match.

San Francisco police wanted to know if Sells was responsible for the disappearance of 13-year-old Ilene Misheloff. She vanished without a trace as she walked home from school on January 30, 1989. They could uncover no clear connection to the man behind bars in Texas.

Then there was the case of 40-year-old Thomas Brose. He, too, worked the carnival circuit. On April 15, 1998, his body was found in his motor home at the Marina Motel on Roosevelt Avenue in the south side of San Antonio. Based on an identification of Sells' picture by a landlord in the Rio Grande Valley, the family of the victim believes Brose rented an apartment for other carnival workers, including Sells, in Mercedes, Texas, and that Sells moved with the carnival to San Antonio, where he shot Brose to death. San Antonio law enforcement, however, did not consider Sells a suspect. And, after initially agreeing with Brose's family that he was responsible for the murder, Sells more recently said that he was in Del Rio all that month.

But Lieutenant Larry Pope still wondered. "There's a lot to indicate he did that one. He said a lot of things that really matched up. But he said he doesn't want to tell about it 'cause they [the State of Texas] 'll give you the death penalty."

In pursuit of corroborating evidence for some of the others, it was time for Tommy Lynn Sells to take his confessional on the road. In March, Rangers Allen and Smith made the arrangements for a visit to Arkansas, Idaho and Nevada.

CHAPTER TWENTY-EIGHT

THE Rangers, Sells and two pilots flew off in the Department of Public Safety's aircraft. Before they could go to any crime scenes, though, there was one additional stop to make. A small oil leak had been found in the plane during its annual check-up. The pilots needed to make a stop in Oklahoma City, the closest location where they could find mechanics capable of repairing that plane.

The Rangers and their prisoner sat in the lounge of the repair shop. Two men with guns and a man in handcuffs created an uncomfortable time for all involved. Any distraction was a welcome diversion. They watched the coffee supply truck pull into the lot with uncommon interest. The woman driving the truck maintained their attention as she performed the mundane task of unloading supplies. They watched as she waved to the men who had helped her and jumped into the truck. All eyes were on her when she backed her vehicle up and ran into their plane. She hit one wing, bending up the tip so that it pointed straight to the sky. In that small fender-bender, she did a total of $25,000 to $30,000 worth of damage. They were now stranded before their trip had really begun.

The pilots booked flights with Southwest Airlines and headed back to Austin. It wasn't quite as simple for the Rangers. As Coy Smith put it, "To get a prisoner on a commercial flight and wear a gun, I'd rather nearly walk back to Texas."

Johnny Allen negotiated with the coffee company. Their insurance policies would cover most of the cost of the remainder of the Rangers' exploratory trip; the company would cover the rest. Oklahoma Executive Jet Charters was hired, and they flew to Arkansas.

THE stop in Little Rock started out looking like a waste of time. Local authorities had no record of a homicide in 1982 at the house Sells pointed out. But when Lieutenant Terry Ward of the Little Rock Police Department contacted the homeowner to see if he had any recollection of any unusual event, he did. It had happened to his tenant, only he did not die. He fell to the ground and played dead as Sells pulled the trigger.

Sells then led investigators and the crew of *48 Hours* down tiny country roads to the blue hole where he claimed to have left a woman's body after he raped her. Local authorities, though, did not want to expend the funds necessary for an expensive underwater search to locate her body. That was where the mystery ended. Her name unknown. Her death uncertain.

THE next stop was Twin Falls, Idaho. There, Sells led investigators to the site of a 1997 murder. He confessed to raping and killing a long-haired blonde woman, chopping her body up with an axe and burying her on the banks of the Snake River.

The Snake River winds as sinuously as its namesake through the canyon it has carved over eons. It is a place of excruciating, yet forbidding, beauty. The crevice it has etched is so deep, cameramen had to lean close to the edge to glimpse the descent down to the canyon floor. Without hesitation, Sells led them to a well-hidden path that led down the canyon wall.

He remarked that everything looked a lot different than it did before. When he pointed out the spot where he buried his victim, there was one problem. Two years before, a massive landslide had occurred in that spot pushing the burial site into the river itself. Any attempt at recovery would be difficult, if not impossible.

Sells' recollection of the woman who died there was

so clear that a forensic artist was brought into the case. Shirley Timmons, the same woman who'd worked with Krystal Surles when she described her attacker, worked with Sells to create a likeness of the blonde.

When Sells and Timmons met, he leaned across the table close to her, looked her in the eye and asked, "You was the one that drew that picture that got me caught, weren't you?"

"Yes, I am."

"I didn't think it was all that good."

For a moment, Timmons did not respond. Then she mirrored Sells' body language and said, "It was good enough to get you caught, wasn't it?"

When the sketch aired on *America's Most Wanted*, Lisa Mueller recognized her daughter, Yvette. In 1997, Yvette had gone to a convenience store to make a phone call. She never returned.

There was one glitch in this identification, though. Yvette Mueller was kidnapped in Las Vegas. Sells' recollection placed the victim at a convenience store in Twin Falls, where he had also stolen a brown station wagon. He also thought the woman had been hitchhiking from Canada to Salt Lake City. Authorities could verify that a vehicle matching that description was stolen in the area at that time. They just didn't know how to fit Yvette into the puzzle.

All agreed it was possible that she had been kidnapped and killed in the Las Vegas area by Sells, and that another woman was killed outside of Twin Falls. It was also possible that the two were the same woman.

"He's been off by a few cities and by two or three years on homicides. But he's never been off by states before," said Ranger Smith. Still, he admitted, with the number of murders Sells had committed, and the amount of drugs he'd abused, anything was possible.

THE traveling investigation team then flew to Winnemucca, Nevada. In the police department's interview room, Sells sat with his back to a window wall. Across the table from him, the Rangers had a clear view of the room behind the glass. It was filled with members of the Winnemucca Police Department, the county sheriff's department and the FBI.

They listened as Sells described Stefanie Stroh's jewelry, her clothing, the bag she carried, where she had been and where she was going. Eyes bulged and grins spread with each revelation. Occasionally, high fives erupted in celebration. They had Sells dead to rights, and they knew it.

They made preparations for him to lead them to the body. Before departure, it was necessary to frisk the prisoner. Sells, already irate at the lack of respect shown to him by the FBI, blew up when the jailer accidentally—or purposely—pulled his hair. Sells lunged at him, hands on his throat. Tall, muscular Texas Ranger Smith was on Sells in a heartbeat, roughly subduing the smaller man.

When tempers cooled, the search for Stefanie's body began anew. They drove past an abandoned building, unrecognizable in its state of total dilapidation. Sells correctly described it as a former truck stop. He led the crew to a desolate spot in the desert. Sells said that, because he was angry about his treatment in Winnemucca, he had intentionally taken them to the wrong spot. The Rangers thought it was possible that Sells had deliberately misled them, but were dismayed that a thorough search of the area never occurred.

Four bodies were sought on this road trip—only one was found, and that one was still alive.

A sullen Sells returned to Del Rio. On the eighth of June in Fayette County Circuit Court in Kentucky, Reba and Michael McHone filed suit against Tommy Lynn Sells on behalf of the estate of their daughter, Haley. She was described in the complaint as "[. . .] a vibrant teenager, full of life and spirit with shoulder-length blonde hair and beautiful green eyes."

Count one alleged that she was innocently playing on the swings when she was abducted, seized, kidnapped, falsely imprisoned, assaulted, tortured, maimed, mutilated, raped and killed by Tommy Lynn Sells. "The Young Teenager was thereafter humiliated, ridiculed, held up to scorn, embarrassed, placed in a false light and slandered by the Defendant."

They requested punitive damages for her pain and suffering, lost earnings potential and funeral costs. In addition, they sought damages to the parents for loss of love and affection of a child. They cited that Sells had hidden the body knowing it would create panic and cause suffering to her parents and others. "The deranged Defendant, on information and belief, had previously killed 13 men and women going back to 1981 and was thereby well aware of actions or inactions which would aid and abet him in continuing the course of conduct which he had in this matter, and evidenced a cruel callous heart and inhuman characteristics which animals themselves do not evidence among their various species." No amount of damages was specified.

Thomas C. Chupak, the court-appointed Guardian Ad Litem for Sells, responded with a request that the plaintiff be denied and the complainant dismissed because of his incarceration and impending trial in Texas and because the complainant had failed to state a case upon which relief could be granted. Sells submitted a hand-written response to the court. In it, he said he could not be in Lexington, Kentucky, to defend himself because of his situation in Texas. He also complained that he could not read the name of his guardian on the document sent and did not know how to contact him.

IN the Val Verde Correctional Center on June 25, 2000, Sells and Danny Calderon in the adjoining cell talked about religion and forgiveness through the bean holes in their doors.

"I'm depressed about being in jail," Danny confessed.

"Then you should just hang yourself," Sells said.

"If I did that, Tommy, God would not forgive me."

"Once you give your life to God, he forgives you. Period."

"I don't think so. You have to ask forgiveness for everything you do wrong," Calderon countered.

"You stupid sack of shit, where did you get that fucking idea?"

"It says so in the Bible. And when you kill yourself, you're dead. You can't ask for forgiveness for that anymore," Danny answered.

"You're a punk. Get in your bunk," Sells ordered.

"You can't tell me what to do in my own cell."

"Oh, yeah? I'm gonna make you my punk. And then I'm going to kill you."

"You won't kill me, Tommy. But you should ask God for forgiveness for saying that."

"I'm gonna poke out your eyes and kill you slowly. Just wait till they open this door."

No matter what Calderon said after this point, Sells continued to rage, "I'm gonna kill you."

Calderon filed an incident report about these threats. He was moved to another cell away from Sells. But no charges were filed and no disciplinary action was taken.

ALLEN and Smith continued to be amazed by their prisoner after months of interviews. "In Tommy, you've got a petty thief and a burglar," Smith explained. "You've got some of the traits of Ted Bundy and Henry Lee Lucas. And to cap it all off, you've got the artistic ability of some of the nation's top con artists who swindle companies and people out of billions of dollars every year. You've got all that clumped up in one guy, one person.

"He can completely cripple an investigator in a small town trying to investigate a fifteen-year-old murder, and the guy goes out the door shaking his head. And he'll do it all because, 'I ain't got nothing better to do.'

"One day, he can be stealing $30 out of the kitty. The next day he can be beating a whole family to death. And the next day, he can be sitting down here in Del Rio fixing the air conditioner of your car.

"It's every criminal in one neat human package. He represents a small part of society that [. . .] I don't think many in law enforcement have ever recognized. He is a terrorist in society. He preys, hit and run, devoted to self-gratification, self-preservation."

Throughout these months, the Texas Rangers were faced with a dilemma. They desperately wanted to close as many cases as possible to bring closure to families. First of all, they wanted to track down the nameless victims of Tommy Lynn Sells. Their experience in Texas gave them a logical answer: When he confesses to one of these murders, contact the central missing persons clearinghouse for that state and match the victim to the crime. To their dismay, they discovered that not every state had one. Even if they narrowed the search to a particular area, and called the most probable county, it didn't always work. If a body were found just one hundred feet on the wrong side of the county line, the agency they contacted would not be aware of it.

Second, they wanted to alert all law enforcement agencies across the country about the serial killer in their possession. ViCAP seemed a simple solution, but it was far from ideal for a killer who operated like Sells.

"It wants to put everybody in a category," said Coy Smith.

Johnny Allen added, "And you won't get a hit unless you put in that."

"In other words," Smith explained, "you've got one killer who cuts all the women with an eight-inch-blade hunting knife in the throat—it's a chain—it'll give you something. But if you've got a guy like Sells who goes and beats this one, cuts this one's throat, shoots this one, then there's no connection, so you don't know."

There seemed to be only one viable alternative to their problem, the national media. They would not have a problem finding a willing outlet—their phones had been ringing with media calls since Sells' arrest. But they did not want to do anything that would compromise the upcoming trial in Del Rio. So they chose to work with *48 Hours*, the only group who agreed not to air anything until after the trial.

The long hours of confession, negotiation and coordination took an emotional and physical toll on the Rangers. But they were about to get a break. It was show time for Tommy Lynn Sells in the Val Verde County Courthouse.

CHAPTER TWENTY-NINE

JURY selection began on August 22, 2000, in the 63rd Judicial District Courtroom of the Val Verde Justice Center in Del Rio. The court summoned five hundred county residents—more than double their usual number—to jury duty.

Thomas F. Lee, District Attorney, entered the courtroom bearing the mantle of an anointed angel of justice. Assistant District Attorney Fred Hernandez was at his side, equally determined to bring the wrath of the State down on the head of Tommy Lynn Sells. The outcome of this case mattered a great deal to both these men. Lee was running in an election for county judge. Hernandez sought Lee's current job as D.A. A result of death by lethal injection would guarantee life for their political futures.

On the other side of the courtroom was court-appointed defense attorney Victor Roberto Garcia, Bobby to his friends. Thinning gray hair framed a round face with warm, dark eyes, giving him the look of everyone's favorite uncle.

Sells entered the courtroom. Gone were the long hair, full beard and tattered jeans he had worn when he was arrested. In his blue suit, white shirt and wire-rimmed glasses, he was well-groomed and looked more like a studious bookworm than a cold-blooded killer. The only indication that he was not what he seemed was a blue tattoo of a rose blooming on his neck just above the edge of his shirt collar.

The three attorneys examined one hundred and twenty members of the jury pool. In legal terms, this body is referred to as the venire—each individual in the group as a venire member. Many were eliminated because they were unshakably convinced of Sells' guilt, or because they thought a life sentence was too lenient and they would always give a death sentence to anyone convicted of murder. Others were sent home because of their opposition to the death penalty. Some did not gain a seat because they believed that if you kill once, you will kill again. One juror was excused because he was not a citizen of the United States and another because he was the brother-in-law of the defense attorney.

According to defense team notes, venire member number one did not feel that the death penalty was used enough or properly. His father, who had been a drug runner, had been murdered in 1977. A bodyguard killed him for drugs and money, but only received a nine-month sentence. The defense challenged him and was sustained by the judge.

Of potential juror number six, the defense noted, "This girl is stoned." Before the seventeenth candidate was questioned, the judge embarked on a nine-minute discourse about special issues and other elements of the law. The monologue was not recorded by the court reporter. Throughout it all, the woman in the box was attentive, but would not look at the defendant. The defense challenged her for an inability to follow the law. She was dismissed.

While the thirteenth prospect was being questioned, mitigation specialist Vince Gonzales noted: "Tommy has passed a note saying he is starting to get pissed. A lawyer from Uvalde is sitting in the gallery staring at Tommy. About this time, 9:57 A.M., Donna and Jessica came in. Tommy calms down some." Donna Hughes was an employee of the aviation firm that had come to the rescue of the downed Texas Rangers and Tommy Lynn Sells in Oklahoma. She had kept in touch with Sells since then— even buying his suits for the trial.

Defense notes said that venire member twenty-four was an "IDIOT" who "misunderstands the difference between probability and possibility with possibility being more likely than not." He was not the only potential juror with confusion on this issue.

Number thirty-seven claimed she was unemployed, yet she listed a work number on her questionnaire. She stated that she had learned a lot from *Unsolved Mysteries*, but swore she did not have a TV and did not believe in cable.

Sells passed another note to Gonzales. "See I messed up my family, Mom, Tim, Jim, Randy. I believe beyond fixing. God blessed me with another family and I messed that up as well. That's what got me into this mess."

A mutual challenge was made to dismiss venire member forty. He was an emergency room nurse who had treated Krystal Surles during her brief stopover at Val Verde Medical Center. He was also the one who had drawn blood from Sells for testing after his arrest.

Potential juror number forty-two seemed to have followed the case with an abnormal intensity. He also admitted to multiple viewings of *The Faces of Death*, a controversial video filled with images of actual deaths of real people.

The State challenged venire member forty-six because he did not think Tommy Lynn Sells was capable of committing this crime. The State's challenge was denied, but he was excused after a peremptory strike.

The defense wrote, "This woman is a Neo-Nazi" about potential juror number seventy-seven. They challenged her because she believed the defense had to present evidence of innocence. The challenge was upheld.

Of number seventy-nine, they wrote, "Mormon— Blood Atonement!" They challenged him for being combative and evasive, but the judge denied them. They needed to use one of their peremptory strikes, a defense team's one tool for unilaterally disqualifying potential jurors.

Sells commented to Garcia on his notepad. "You will be a hated man before this is over with."

"I was hated the day I took your case but that is okay. I don't care. If they get in trouble, they will want somebody like me who is not a nice guy," he responded.

"You are a nice guy. I have never not liked you."

"Thanks but I mean they want somebody that can fight in court and not lie down."

"It's me I don't like."

"I can't help that," Garcia wrote.

While potential juror number 105 was on the stand, Sells scratched a note to Gonzales, "Low Blow. Judge called Bobby a balloon-headed man."

In a capital case, selection of a jury is a high-stakes game. Inevitably, contention arose. Garcia requested the opportunity to question all the potential jurors about their attitudes on parole. He asserted that the jurors had a right to know that if they gave Sells a life sentence, he would have to serve a minimum of forty years' imprisonment before he would be eligible for parole. Judge George Thurmond denied his request. Garcia raised this objection repeatedly throughout the process.

Sells sent a note covering the front of three green Post-it notes to Jessica:

> I'm afraid. I'm not afraid of this court. I'm afraid I won't have you no more. I know you keep telling me I don't have nothing to worry over. I'm just afraid.
>
> I feel like going crazy. Do you want to come with me? I will try to call again tonight, 7 to 9. I'm sorry I could not call last night till so late. But I did try. Will you try and call the sheriff and see if we can have lunch at the same time at the jail? Love you.
>
> Bobby keeps trying to tell me I don't need to be looking at you or talking with you. Because other people don't like it. I keep telling him, Oh well, I love you so I can't keep from it.

Jessica's response covered the backs of the sheets Sells sent. She added one additional page that she covered front and back.

Tommy, XOXOXOXO Please believe me you
don't have anything to worry about. I love you. I
will always be there no matter what happens. Just
promise me you will stay with me no matter what.
Nothing's wrong, baby. I promise. I'm just trying
to be patient waiting for the Lord to do something
or show me what he's gonna do.

I'm just here holding on just like you and hon-
estly pray I never lose you. I love you! You know
even your mom knows that. That's why she
doesn't wonder about me. I just wonder why you
don't want me to do anything with your brother.
You know if he was going to stay with me also.
Did you think he was going to hurt me? I know
it's not jealousy. Ha! Ha! He doesn't even like me.
Ha! Ha! But anyway, you have nothing to worry
about. I love you. Your wife, Jessie.

For fourteen tiresome days, the prosecution and the
defense repeated the same questions to one member of the
jury pool after another. Finally, the chosen twelve, plus two
alternates, were impaneled.

Seated on the jury were: Miriam Gonzales; Hilda
Loper, who worked for a justice of the peace office and a
local law firm; James Jones, retired military—both Navy
and Air Force; William Cooper, a Taoist with two years in
law school; Jay Hayden; Aida Victoria Gomez, whose husband was a state trooper; Eleanor A. Stark, at 71, the oldest
member of the jury, and a retired U.S. Customs worker;
Anna Riegel; Mark Rivas; Dwight Brown; William Grady
King; and Pedro Vidales, who had said at one point during
questioning, "If you kill once, you'll kill again," and
claimed not to have understood the judge's question regarding independent assessment of the evidence. The defense had used up all its peremptory strikes by the time
Vidales was seated. They pleaded with the judge for additional peremptories, but were denied.

After they were sworn in, Sells stuck a pink Post-it

note in front of Garcia. "Do you want me to retract everything I said?"

Then he wrote an explanation of himself to Jessica.

There was a boy who grew up lost to this world. Never knew where to go. Never knew where to turn.

The boy grew up to be a man. Well, somewhat of one. But he never knew where to go and still's lost to this world.

He fell in love. Oh how good his heart felt. How special she was to him. Always had a warm touch to offer him. But he was lost to this world.

She gave and gave. He took and took. He tried his best to give back. But you see he was lost to this world.

He grew up lean and mean.

The trial was scheduled to start in a few days on September 12. It was expected to last two weeks.

CHAPTER THIRTY

THE small town of Del Rio transformed into a media Mecca overnight. Traveling 160 miles west of San Antonio, many of the out-of-town journalists felt they'd come to the end of the earth.

The reporters, cameras and mobile studios surrounded the historic building downtown. Built in 1887, it is the only courthouse Val Verde County has ever known.

On the first day of the trial, the star of the show was not the man whose life or death would be decided on the second floor of the courthouse. It was the young survivor, Krystal Surles. Cameras zoomed in to catch a glimpse of the puckered scar slashed across her neck. She smiled and waved to the cameras as she entered the building.

When the judge entered the courtroom, Sells wrote a note to his attorney. "9-12-2000!! Started the trial!! 9:02 A.M. You said to look at the twelve when we stand up. I feel pretty helpless here. You need to do something."

"Look at the person reading the indictment," Garcia responded. "When you answer, look at the jury."

Assistant D.A. Fred Hernandez stood to read the charges. When Tommy Lynn Sells stood to respond, the gallery greeted him with short gasps and drawn out hisses.

Count one accused, "[. . .] in the course of committing burglary of a habitation with intent to commit aggravated assault, did then and here intentionally commit murder by causing the death of an individual, Kaylene Harris by cutting the throat of Kaylene Harris with a knife."

"How does the defendant plead to that accusation, guilty or not guilty?" the judge intoned.

"Not guilty," Sells responded.

Count two charged that he committed an aggravated sexual assault and caused the death of Kaylene Harris. Once again, he said, "Not guilty."

Count three claimed Tommy Lynn Sells "[. . .] did then and there attempt to cause the death of an individual, Krystal Surles, by cutting the throat of said Krystal Surles with a knife, which act was more than the mere preparation but failed to accomplish the murder of Krystal Surles against the peace and dignity of the State."

"And to this accusation, the defendant pleads?"

"Guilty," Sells said to the surprise of the court and the spectators alike.

"The defendant may have his seat. We're ready to proceed, then, with the opening statement. Does the State desire to be heard?"

"Yes, Your Honor. Good morning, ladies and gentlemen. As most of you remember, my name is Freddy Hernandez, and I'm the assistant district attorney. I think most of you saw me during the individual *voir dire* process. And seated at the table is Mr. Tom Lee, the district attorney, and we're here today for one reason, to see that justice is done."

After explaining the purpose of his opening statement to the jury, he summarized the State's case. "You are going to hear evidence about this horrible case. You are going to hear how the defendant, Tommy Lynn Sells, knew the victim and her family. They are going to tell you how, before December thirty-first of 1999, they knew Tommy Lynn Sells, where they knew him from, how they befriended him. In fact, they had even bought an automobile from him at his work place. That is what they are going to testify about.

"They are going to get on the stand and they are going to tell you that Tommy Sells, the defendant, had been in their home on various occasions and spoken to both of the Harrises, and also knew the kids, including Kaylene. [. . .] The Harrises are going to tell you where their home is located [. . .] outside the city limits of Del Rio just past

Amistad Lake as you cross the bridge going to Sanderson. It is a fairly isolated area. It is dark and the houses are far apart. They are going to tell you if you want to get to their house, you actually have to make an effort to get to their house. You are not just going to be driving by the house randomly.

"[. . .] Terry Harris is going to tell you on the evening of December thirtieth of 1999, he saw the defendant, Tommy Sells. He saw him at what used to be the Quickie Mart next to Ram Country, and on that day Terry Harris and some friends were going to Kansas. They had their luggage in his truck, and the defendant said, 'Hey, are you going somewhere? Where are you going?' and Terry Harris told him, 'I'm taking a trip up north,' so that defendant at that point in time knew the man of the house was going to be gone.

"[. . .] Most importantly, you are going to hear from the brave little girl who is going to tell you how she survived the brutal attack inflicted by the defendant. She's going to walk you step by step through each and every detail of what she saw and what she heard on the early morning hours of December thirty-first, 1999."

Hernandez ran through a list of other witnesses and their anticipated testimony: Texas Ranger John Allen; Val Verde County Sheriff's Department Investigator Larry Pope; Dr. Jan Garavaglia, Bexar County pathologist; and Dr. Cynthia Beamer, a physician in San Antonio who had treated Krystal Surles.

"There will be one DNA expert that will be called, a serologist that will tell you the defendant's blood, along with Katy's blood, was found on his clothes. Another expert who compares fibers will tell you that his fibers were all over the victim's clothes and the victim's fibers were all over his clothes as well, showing contact.

"Ladies and gentlemen, this is a horrible crime, and at the end of the guilt–innocence, we are going to ask that you find the defendant, Tommy Lynn Sells, guilty of capital murder."

• • •

DEFENSE Attorney Garcia began by admitting, "This is a horrible case. It is a brutal case, and I told you that. You come in here because all twelve of you said you could be fair, that you had an open mind, and that if you had any opinions, that those would not affect or influence how you looked at this case, and now you understand how critical it is.

"Tommy Lynn Sells came in here today and he pled guilty to the attempted murder of [. . .] Krystal Surles. He told you that. That's the first part of accepting some responsibility for what has been explained to you. The second part is he pled not guilty to capital murder."

Then Garcia reached the crux of the defense: the evidence for capital murder does not exist. There was no burglary—nothing was taken from the Harris home except the screens from two windows. There was no intent to commit sexual assault.

"Never in those confessions [. . .] beginning on January second does he ever talk about 'My intent to go into the Harrises' trailer was to commit aggravated sexual assault.' It never was. You may hear evidence that says, 'I don't know why, but I was.' He is not going to deny that he was inside that trailer, and hasn't from day one."

Garcia continued to explain that it wasn't until five days after his arrest that Sells admitted to touching Kaylene's genitals, because he was told that that confession would get him the death penalty. And, at that point, Tommy Lynn Sells wanted to die.

In closing, Garcia said, "We're not sidestepping responsibility. We're not sidestepping what happened. Tommy Lynn Sells has accepted responsibility for what he did, and I ask you for you to keep an open mind as to that portion of the case. Thank you."

When Garcia was seated, he had this note from his client: "The guy with the long hair by the man with the red shirt has a hole in his neck."

"Tracheotomy scar. It's surgical. He will be sympathetic with Krystal Surles," he responded.

"You would have had fun if I had not talked," Sells jotted.

"I might have gotten you off," was the reply.

THE first witness called by the prosecution was Noel Houchin, an employee of Larry's Lakeside Tavern.

"He just blatantly asked me for sex," she said. "I promptly turned him down."

"Okay. You have said 'blatantly'; do you recall what he might have said to you?" Hernandez asked.

" 'Will you have sex with me?' "

"And what was your response?"

"I said, 'Thank you, but no.' "

"Did any of that continue?"

Noel rolled her eyes. "All night long. It never stopped."

"Describe to us how that may have continued through the evening," Hernandez requested.

"[. . .] I told him that my car was broke down. He offered to go and check out my car for me if I would have sex with him. He offered to pay to have it fixed for me if I would have sex with him. He then told me that he owned Amigo Motors and that I could have my pick of any vehicle on the lot if I would have sex with him."

"And what were your responses when he made these different offers to you?"

"I tried to stay as polite as possible. I told him, 'Thank you, but no, I have a boyfriend.' I told him repeatedly that I wasn't in the habit of getting paid for sex."

"What was his reaction?"

"He just continued to ask over and over. He never seemed upset about it, just kept asking more," she said.

"Did you all talk about anything else?"

"No. Not really. He [. . .] finally got around to asking me for just five minutes of my time."

"Okay. And when you mean he asked for five minutes of your time, explain to us what you mean."

"He [. . .] kept telling me that five minutes was all he needed, just five minutes of my time, just five minutes."

"And how did you respond?"

"I just said, 'No, thank you.' I was being polite in as many possible ways as I could."

"Did he ever ask you anything else?"

"Oh, he asked where I lived, several times," Noel said.

"Did you tell him where you lived?"

"No, sir, I did not."

"Why didn't you tell him where you lived?"

"I thought it was kind of unusual that it would be so consistent, constantly asking over and over again for sex, and I didn't feel comfortable telling him where I lived."

"Did you give him any idea where you lived?"

"Yes, he asked me how long it took to get home, and I told him, 'Approximately five minutes.' "

"How long did Tommy Lynn Sells stay there at Larry's Bar?"

"He stayed until [. . .] 2:15 A.M."

The whole time Noel was on the stand, Sells furiously wrote notes and whispered to his attorney. In his mind, the only truth she told was that he was at Larry's Bar that night. He scribbled "Lie, Lie, Lie" all over his legal pad.

FOLLOWING the barmaid's testimony, the jury heard from three members of the Harris family. Crystal Harris was the first one of them to take the stand. Her face hung haggard with the pain of her recent loss. Her eyes seemed focused inward, rerunning the memory tape of her daughter, Kaylene.

When asked how she met Sells, she said, "We met him in church, and when my husband and I decided to buy our car, our truck, we decided to go to somebody who had a dealership through our church, to help them out, and we met Tommy there and also at church."

"What church was that?"

"Grace Community Church."

"Now, prior to December the thirty-first of 1999, had

the defendant been to your home or visited your home?"

"Yes," Crystal answered.

"Do you recall how many occasions he had gone to your home?"

"About three occasions that I'm aware of."

"Do you know what the nature of his visits were?"

"He came to talk to my husband about marital problems and problems with his job."

Hernandez asked her, "Had he seen your children when he had gone to your home?"

"Yes," she answered.

"Including Kaylene?"

"Yes."

"Did he ever play with the dog that was in State's Exhibit Number Sixteen?"

"Yes, he did."

"And explain to us how that occurred."

"On one occasion when he was at our home, the kids wanted to take the dog on a walk and Tommy helped them put the harness on the dog. The kids took the dog on a walk and played with him in the front yard, and he [Sells] was very happy. The dog liked him."

As Terry Harris took the stand, Sells' pen flashed across his notepad, "Terry Harris. Nail his ass!!! He's a punk. A want-to-be."

Harris testified about his relationship with Sells and their encounter before Terry left Del Rio for Kansas. When Garcia did not question him about cocaine, Sells wrote, "You may know what you're doing but I want to know what you're doing."

"I want to cover better when we call Terry back up," Garcia wrote back.

Sells continued writing. "What's the point in telling Jessica about sex with the bartender? What's the point in telling her to seek power of attorney? What do you mean we're going to call her Friday?"

Then, Justin Harris, Crystal's blind son, took the stand

to recount the events that had occurred in his room the night Katy died. His testimony locked in the time frame of the crime. He told the court that he awoke before his clock was scheduled to ring at 4:30 A.M. and went to the bathroom. Before he could return to his bed, someone else shut off his alarm.

The judge and the attorneys then discussed the ramifications of Sells' guilty plea to the attempted murder of Krystal Surles. The possibility of a life sentence and a fine of $10,000 was mentioned by Judge Thurmond. In response, Sells fired off an angry note to his lawyer: "You really need to start letting me know more. On this shit with the Judge today and a $10,000 fine? You told me 5 to 20." Concerned that his wife would have to cover any fine assessed on him, he wrote, "You have to understand this: Jessica is all I have. Don't mess this up."

CHAPTER THIRTY-ONE

THE State's star witness, Krystal Surles, took the stand after a recess for lunch. Sells requested to be absent from the courtroom during her testimony. But the judge insisted that he be there.

A breathless courtroom watched as the young girl, clad in a striped shirt, stepped up to testify. Her blonde hair, pulled back in a ponytail, revealed a face that was grim and determined. All eyes were on her pink badge of courage, a scar stretching from one side of her neck to the other.

Hernandez opened slowly. "How was it that you ended up staying with the Harrises?"

"Because my mom's fiancé met him, because they are interested in the same things."

"So you knew the Harrises through your mom and her fiancé?"

She nodded energetically, her ponytail bobbing behind her. Hernandez reminded her that the court reporter needed an audible answer for the record. "Now, I would like to take you back, if I could, to December thirtieth of 1999, and ask you if you remember being at the Harrises' on that particular date."

"Yes," she answered, a small cloud passing over her eyes.

"Do you remember what you may have been doing early in the day, or throughout the day?"

"Planning a New Year's Eve party."

"And when you say, 'Planning a New Year's Eve party,' " Hernandez asked, "who was planning a party?"

"Me, Katy and Lori."

"Now when you say the name *Katy*, are you referring to Kaylene Harris?"

"Yes."

"Katy was just a nickname that her family called her, and her friends, right?"

"Yes."

"What sort of party were you all going to have? What sort of party were you planning?"

"Just have friends over, so I could meet them before school started again," she answered.

After easing her through the preliminaries, Hernandez moved her back to that dark memory—into the bedroom that she still feared. "Were you ever awakened during the night?" he asked.

"Yes."

"What was it that awakened you?"

"Katy's voice saying 'Help,' " she replied.

"Now when you were awakened, did you notice whether there was any light, or whether it was dark, or— What were the lighting conditions like?"

"It was—The light was on."

"And what did you notice or hear Katy say, if anything?"

Krystal fidgeted in her seat. "I couldn't understand what she was saying, what she was trying to say, stuff."

"Was there some reason why you couldn't understand what she was saying?"

"Because his hand was over her mouth," she answered.

"Whose hand was over her mouth?"

A tiny, trembling finger containing the power of life and death rose in the air and pointed across the courtroom to Tommy Lynn Sells. "His hand," she said.

"The man in the blue jacket and glasses?"

"Yes." She stared hard at Sells, but his gaze remained transfixed on the surface of the desk. He would not raise his head and meet her eyes.

"God help me here," Sells wrote. "I'm falling apart. Help me. All I know to do is hang my head. I hate this."

"Let the record reflect that the witness has identified the defendant, Tommy Lynn Sells," Hernandez noted. "Now, Krystal, if you need for me to stop at some point in time, I'll stop. Describe to us what you saw when you opened your eyes and you were telling us you saw Katy and the defendant."

"The position they were in?" she asked.

"Well, tell us what you saw, yes."

"Okay. He was standing behind her with his hand over her mouth and the knife right here." She mimed holding a knife up to her own throat.

"So he had a knife in his hand?"

Krystal nodded and said, "Yes."

Hernandez had Krystal make a drawing of the room and put marks for the positions of all the players while he continued his questioning. "Now, describe to us what the defendant was doing with Katy at that point in time. You want to have a seat?"

She sat down and her eyes darted left to right in confusion. "Can you repeat the question?"

"When you saw Katy and the defendant standing over here where you have drawn, on the drawing that you have made, what was the defendant doing, and what was Katy doing?"

"Katy was—He was . . ." Krystal's face crumbled and her sobs echoed through the silent, intent courtroom. The court took a brief recess.

"Help, Jessica. I pray you are praying for me," Sells scratched on the paper.

When they returned, Hernandez resumed his questioning. "We had been discussing the layout of the room that you [. . .] said that Katy had slept in that night. When you opened your eyes, you said, you saw Katy and the defendant standing sort of in a corner of the room, is that correct?"

"Yes."

"Okay. Can you describe to us what was going on at that point in time?"

"He had his hand over her mouth and the knife like this." Once again Krystal raised her imaginary knife up to her neck.

"When you say 'he,' you are referring to the defendant?"

"Yes."

"What did Katy do? What was she doing, if anything?"

"She was struggling." Rays of pain radiated from Krystal's small face and touched everyone in the courtroom.

"Did she do anything else?"

"She told me—She told me with her eyes to stay there and not move, just to lay there, and so I did."

"So what did you do?"

"I laid there. Oh, yeah, I laid there, but I still—I still could see. I laid there."

At the prosecuting attorney's request, Krystal rose from the witness stand and got on his desk to demonstrate how she was lying down on the bed.

"Was there anything else on the top bunk?" he asked her.

"No."

"Were there any railings or anything?"

"Oh, yeah," she smiled as she corrected herself, "there were railings, yeah."

"So how much were you able to see from the top bunk as you were laying down like you just showed us? Were you able to see very much?"

"No. I only could kind of see from here," she placed her hand on her upper chest, "and up."

"So you saw Katy's head and up, and the defendant's head and up?"

"Yes."

"Did you stay in the top bunk the entire time as you were observing what was going on?"

"Yes."

"What happened after Katy motioned with her eyes to you to stay still? What did you do?"

"I just stayed there and watched."

"What happened next?"

Her lip quivered, her eyes overflowed with pain. "He moved the knife and slit her throat."

The emotion of Krystal's testimony wafted through the gallery. More than her family and friends were affected. Curious onlookers, court officials and desensitized members of the media were all feeling the tightening of a lump in the throat.

"Fred has no heart pushing Krystal," Sells wrote.

Hernandez continued. "And then what? How did Katy react, or what happened to Katy?"

"She just fell."

"Did she just fall down, anything in particular?"

"She turned and grabbed the poster and fell."

At Hernandez's instruction, Krystal stood, and walked across the room to demonstrate what she had just described.

"Did Katy do anything else after you saw her fall?"

"She started making really bad noises."

"And when you say 'bad noises,' " Hernandez asked, "how would you describe them?"

"She was gasping for air, but she couldn't get any because there was all this blood, and it was just a really gurgling, icky sound."

She returned to her diagram to point out the position of Katy's body. When she took her seat, Hernandez asked, "What were you thinking when the man was coming towards you?"

"I was really scared, and I didn't know what to do." Her breathing became shallower as she relived the moment in her mind.

"Did you say anything to him?"

"Yes."

"What did you tell him?"

"I said, 'I won't say nothing, I promise. I'm not making noises. I won't say nothing. I'll be quiet. It's Katy making the noises.' " Her lips twisted and her eyes turned away, welling with tears, as she fought to keep her emotions under control.

"Jessica, I really need your help," Sells scribbled across the paper. "Let's go to heaven. This one's killing me."

"Okay," Hernandez responded. "[. . .] Did he say anything to you after you told him that?"

"He said, 'Move your hands.' " She blinked her eyes shut and held them tightly closed as she swallowed hard.

"And why did he say, 'Move your hands'? Will you show us how you had your hands?"

She put her hands around her neck in a protective position. "I had them up like this."

"You had your hands up on—close to your neck?"

"Yes."

"Can you tell us why you had your hands up close to your neck?"

"Because I saw what he did to Katy, and I was scared he was going to do it to me." Sobs escaped between every word. Krystal trembled uncontrollably, but still persevered.

"And what happened when he got to the top bunk next—where you were at?" Hernandez queried.

"He reached over the ledge and cut my throat," she said in a trembling voice.

"What did you do then?"

"Just laid there and pretended I was dead."

"And tell us why you did that."

"Because if he knew I was alive, he would have come back and killed me for sure." The horror of reliving that moment contorted her face.

Krystal's testimony continued, detailing her flight to the Betzes' home and the arrival of EMS.

"Do you remember anything after that?"

"No," she said, shaking her head as if she could shake loose a memory.

"Now a little while ago, when you said the defendant had cut your throat, do you know what he used to cut you with?"

"A knife."

"And you saw that?"

"Yes."

"The same one that he used to cut Kaylene?"

Her lip quivered, her eyes blinked, she struggled to force out the answer. "Yes."

After a short recess, it was time for cross-examination. Victor Garcia was very brief.

"I just have a couple of questions, Your Honor. Thank you." He turned to address Krystal. "I was not given the opportunity to talk to you before, but I'm really sorry for you having to go through this. You understand that Tommy Sells has pleaded guilty to hurting you?"

"Yes," she whispered.

"You are a brave young woman. Thank you. No more questions."

KRYSTAL is a hero to many who were inside the courtroom and in the world beyond its doors. But Krystal has a list of heroes, too. Chief among them is Herb Betz, a retired military man and the next person to take the stand.

"I opened the door to see why she was there," Herb said.

"And what happened when you opened the door?"

"Well, when I opened the door, with her right hand she was pointing at her throat, and of course she . . ." He cleared his throat to choke down his emotional response. "Once I opened the door, I could tell she was covered with blood from her head all the way to her feet, and with her pointing at her throat, I could see this huge slash across her throat, and her little eyes were just looking at me, saying— seemed to me—saying 'Help me.' "

"He's killing me!!" Sells scratched on his legal pad.

Hernandez asked Betz, "Describe to us the wound, as you saw it, to her throat area."

"Well, the best I can describe it, it was from about here to here," Herb gestured from one side of his neck to the other, "and that's all I could see was the one wound, because there was so much blood and—Well, I guess the windpipe is about this size," he circled his thumb and forefinger together. "And you could see the top part of it and the bottom part of it, because it was completely cut."

"So you were able to physically see the top part and bottom part of the windpipe?"

"Yes, sir." Herb continued on, recounting his time communicating with Krystal that night.

Then Hernandez asked, "What was Krystal's physical condition before EMS arrived?"

"I would say a minute or two before they arrived, Krystal started shaking. She was going into shock."

"And did that last very long?"

"Yeah, long time, even after the paramedics arrived, she was still in shock."

Hernandez asked Herb about the arrival of the paramedics and his discussion with the deputies. Then he asked one final question.

"Did you do anything else?"

"Cried a lot," Betz responded.

The defense had no questions.

But Sells had a complaint. "You said we're doing good. Yeah, right. They're done killed me. You should go now to part two."

CHAPTER THIRTY-TWO

THE next day, trial testimony shifted from emotional presentations to the hard facts. The first witness called was Texas Ranger Johnny Allen. He strode to the stand on his lanky legs. His weatherworn face was chiseled around sharp blue eyes that looked as if they could stare down the sun if it didn't set on time.

"Tell us how you began your questioning, your investigation as far as trying to collect information from Crystal Harris," the prosecutor requested.

"At that point in time, she wasn't fully aware that the body inside was actually Kaylene's body. Of course, she was frantic, in a horrible state of mind emotionally, and I just began trying to ask her questions, like any information she might have that would help us. At that point in time is when we discovered and were told that Terry Harris had left the evening before for Kansas."

Allen related the arrival of the crime-scene techs to process the site, and the hours he spent by their side.

"Were you able to finish the processing of the crime scene on that particular day, the thirty-first?"

"Yes, sir."

"Up until the time that the crime scene had been processed, did you have any type of suspect, or have any idea who had been responsible for what occurred out there?"

"We had not a clue; no, sir, did not."

"What did you do after the crime scene was processed?"

"It lasted several hours, up until, I believe, after dark. By that time Terry Harris had arrived back in Del Rio from

Kansas. We had an interview with Mr. Harris," the Ranger answered.

"Were you able to get any type of information from Mr. Harris that aided you in trying to figure out what had happened out there, who was responsible for it?"

"No, sir, sure was not. Mr. Harris as well was visibly upset, extremely angry and emotional as well."

"So after you interviewed Mr. Harris you still don't have any idea who is responsible?"

"No, sir." Allen then told the jury that after arriving home about midnight, he and Investigator Pope left Del Rio at 5 A.M. the next morning. They headed straight to the forensic center in San Antonio to view the autopsy; then, they went to University Hospital to talk to Krystal Surles.

"How did you begin questioning her or trying to communicate with her?"

"Well, first of all we [. . .] introduced ourselves, explained what we were doing, that we were investigating the crime and that we were just there to try and get any information we could out of her, if it would, you know, be beneficial to our investigation."

"Did she seem to understand—"

"Yes, sir."

"—the questions? How did you proceed after you let her know what you were there for?"

"A lot of questions [. . .] just required a yes or no. She was able to move her head. We first started off trying to get some just general physical description of the suspect, but at that point in time we were aware that she had seen what occurred and apparently did eyewitness the murder and her assault as well." A half grin of admiration dashed across his face as he thought about the brave girl he first met in a hospital bed.

"How were you able to get that information, whatever information you needed in order to continue with your investigation? What did you do?"

"Through questions and answers with Krystal."

"And did you, in fact, make questions, and she provided the answers to you?"

"Correct."

"Now, once you were able to communicate with Krystal via these manners, whether it be with nods or yeses or nos, or she wrote something down, what did you do with that information she provided to you?"

"Of course, we kept written information down that she was able to provide us, and once we finally reached a point where she just about provided all the information she could as far as a general physical description on what his hair length, hair color, facial hair, et cetera, her mother was standing there the whole time, and we walked out into the hallway where Doug Luker, which would have been the fiancé of Krystal's mother, and [. . .] had a conversation with him, interviewed him on any information he could possibly have. At that point in time, I let it be known to him that general description of what Krystal was able to provide for us."

"So up to that point you are telling us that Krystal was able to give you a general description of what she saw, who she saw?"

"I wouldn't say it was a general description," Allen said with a grin. "It was a pretty good description."

"And how was she able to describe him to you?"

"Five-eight, brown hair, beard, past-collar–length hair, Anglo."

Sells wrote to mitigation specialist Vince Gonzales, "The juror in the first row, second seat, looks at me and shakes his head. Green shirt and glasses. Am I supposed to look at them?"

"Yes. But always turn away," Gonzales answered.

After clarifying some details with Hernandez, Allen continued, "Mr. Luker made a comment, it sounds almost as if she's explaining or describing a man that we had talked to at a Diamond Shamrock the evening we were leaving to go to Kansas."

"So it sounded to you like Luker had already seen this person that was being described?"

"Correct. Yes, sir." Allen completed his testimony by detailing the identification of Sells, the preparation of a probable cause affidavit, the procurement of an arrest warrant and the arrest of Tommy Lynn Sells.

"I'm just getting the shit beat out of me," the defendant noted.

LIEUTENANT Larry Pope, investigator for the Val Verde Sheriff's Department, was the next to testify. He had a lean, rangy look and a pugilistic stance. He looked like he'd be far more comfortable chasing down perpetrators on the run than confined in a stuffy courtroom.

He confirmed the statements of Ranger Allen and detailed the handling of the chain of evidence recovered from the scene. He explained the mystery of the bloody footprint on the linoleum. Initially, it was assumed to be Sells' footprint, but when that didn't match, they gathered up shoes from sheriff's department personnel, police officers, DPS techs—from everyone they could place at the scene. Eventually, they found Dexter Tooke, an emergency medical technician who was on the scene that night. It had taken a while because he had changed jobs on January 1. His shoes matched the footprint.

Pope's testimony included only one surprise. It came with this question from Prosecutor Hernandez: "What kind of drugs were found in the Harris trailer?"

He answered, "During the search of the trailer, I found some marijuana residue, a package of rolling papers and a little pipe you can use to smoke marijuana in, and they were inside a saucer."

After his testimony, Sells jotted a note to his attorney. "Pope and Allen said I showed no remorse in the afternoon or that night. I called my mom crying my eyes out."

DR. Jan Garavaglia, Bexar County Medical Examiner, started her testimony with a description of Kaylene's body. "She was a well-developed, well-nourished post-pubertal young white female. She's sixty-three inches in length, five-foot-three, one hundred and fourteen pounds. She looked like she was about thirteen. She's dressed in a kind of over-sized pink tee shirt that's torn on the front. It is blood-soaked. There is multiple defects in the tee shirt. There is a bra beneath the tee shirt, black bra. The clasp is broken on the front, and also there is a stab wound to the front of the bra. No panties are on the body. There is a necklace about the neck with a little dragonfly medallion and a wrist-watch which had the correct time."

Sells noted his impressions of this witness: "Too smart for herself. Lots of big words, smiles a lot as she's talking. All eyes are on her."

"So when you say there were multiple defects to the tee shirt," Hernandez inquired, "can you explain what you mean by that?"

"They corresponded to the stab wounds to the body that she had."

With her testimony, the prosecution submitted one photo after another into evidence. Garcia objected each time, saying that the photographs were "highly prejudicial" and would be presented "merely to inflame the jury and would not be probative in any manner." Judge Thurmond overruled every objection.

Then, Garavaglia began her description of Kaylene's injuries in the neck area. "She's got a five-inch incised wound you could see cut with a sharp force instrument across the neck, almost horizontal. It is five inches across. The lower edge is a sharp, single line. The upper edge is gaping by the time I see it, and it [. . .] looks like she has three separate cuts to the skin, more on the right side. The wound is kind of situated about one-and-a-half inches to the left of the mid-line, extends across the neck, across the right side of the neck almost to behind, a little behind the right ear. She has a thinner neck; everything is smaller with her, you know, because she was a small girl. [. . .]

"The cut extended just above the thyroid cartilage. You would know that as kind of your Adam's apple, so it is just above that. That thyroid cartilage which would be kind of like, you know, our voice box area, that's just kind of hanging open. It is completely cut. In fact, the top portion is cut in half. [. . .] Her carotid artery is cut, and her jugular vein, which is a large vein on the right side, both those are cut on the right side. The left side is not as deep. Now, again, it is cut [. . .] on the right, down to the vertebrae, but on the left, the posterior aspect of the larynx is still there, what we call the pharyngeal muscles, but the right side is cut. The left side is there," she pointed out on the photo, "but behind those, there is another cut, so the knife had to come across and then back in, and it cuts behind that and then actually makes a slit behind those posterior muscles on the left on to the vertebral bodies, which are the vertebrae of the neck."

Pointing to a photograph, she started with the neck area, explaining, "You don't see the carotid and jugular because they contract [. . .] but what is important [. . .]" is that "[. . .] the slit doesn't cut the pharyngeal muscles in the back, but there is another cut beneath the cut, which indicates there is at least one cut across, and then it has to go back behind those muscles and then cut again. There is no way else you can get that." These incisions were one of three fatal injuries inflicted on Kaylene.

"These pictures are killing me. This lady is killing me," Sells complained on paper. Then, in large letters, he wrote, "I don't want to see this shit."

After completing her description of the incisions to her throat, she embarked on a description of the stab wounds to the young girl's body. "She had a total of sixteen stab wounds [. . .] actually nineteen stab defects, sixteen stab wounds with three of those completely going through the body, having an exit defect to it."

Following the order of her examination of the body, she listed them all. "The stab wounds to the upper chest area, you can see there are four of them." Holding up the gruesome autopsy-room photo, she pointed out the injuries one by one. The first two extended deep into the right lung.

The third had crossed the mid-line and then entered the right lung. The fourth penetrated the left lung. "They were so deep that two of them [. . .] appear to go completely through the body and exit the back." The combination of wounds to the lungs was the second fatal injury.

The next stab wound the doctor described is in the upper abdominal region. It passed through the abdominal wall, went through the liver, through the duodenum and about an inch from the stomach. "It is fairly deep. It is, you know, several inches deep. It is going to be about six inches into the abdomen."

She next detailed wounds under the arm, one just above the left hip, and one on the left hip. This one "[. . .] actually hits the bone of the pelvis, stops at the bone and hits it. You can feel the mark on there." She rubbed her finger on that spot on the photograph and continued her grisly tour of stab wounds—pointing out one on the left lateral thigh, another on the upper left arm and the two exit wounds in Kaylene's back.

"The next stab wound [. . .] is mostly horizontal. [. . .] It actually cuts through the renal artery, which is the main blood supply to the kidney on the right. It also cuts the inferior vena cava, and that's the main vein that drains the bottom portion of your body [. . .]. That wound would have been fatal in and of itself."

"This is bad," Sells noted.

Dr. Garavaglia explained the superficial and defensive wounds on Kaylene's hands and arms, including one on the back of the right arm. "That one extends through the arm, actually hits the arm bone and stops at the bone. You can feel the mark on the bone that it left."

She then enumerated the abrasions and contusions on the body. The prosecution put the focus on the two areas that supported their contention of sexual assault. First, Hernandez questioned Dr. Garavaglia on the injuries to Kaylene's legs.

"On the inner aspect of the thigh [. . .]" she said,

"[. . .] is a nice, discreet, oval contusion, and those kind of locations indicate oftentimes grabbing by fingers or thumbs [. . .]. Well, what's unusual about it is, the stab wounds are up here. They are not down on the leg area [. . .] whoever has done this also has an interest in the leg area. I think it is the pattern with the forcible marks on the leg, forcibly torn panties, grabbing of the legs suggests that something else might have been going on."

"God try to hold me still, this had nothing to do with it," Sells wrote.

Assistant D.A. Hernandez then led her up to the victim's genital examination, and Dr. Garavaglia stated, "The acute findings consisted of a very small contusion or bruise [. . .] on the internal aspect of the labia minora [. . .] and then there is [. . .] some reddening. Just where the hymenal ring goes into the labia minora [. . .]." The implication the prosecution wanted the jury to reach was clear—these injuries were a direct result of Sells' finger penetrating Kaylene's vagina.

ON cross-examination, Defense Attorney Garcia asked, "And now in reference to [. . .] Kaylene's genitalia [. . .] can you tell us with a degree of medical certainty [. . .] how that little small contusion got there?"

"No."

"And you also said there was some reddening; this is on the outer area?"

"In that genital region? No, nothing on the outer area. It is all right at the opening of the vagina," Dr. Garavaglia responded.

"But you cannot tell us with any medical certainty how the reddening got there?"

"No, sir."

"You are not telling this jury," Garcia continued, "that it is your opinion that that was done by anything that might have been penetrating?"

"No. I can't say that," she answered.

• • •

HERNANDEZ fired back in re-direct, "I have got two questions. You also can't tell us that it wasn't penetrated, is that correct?"

"Right. I cannot tell what caused that trauma."

"There is trauma," he persisted, "but you can't say whether it was or was not penetrating, is that correct?"

"Oh, definitely. There is no way I could tell."

"And as far as the wounds on the knees and the legs, the bruises, is that consistent with somebody trying to open the legs?"

"That could be a reason, too," Dr. Garavaglia replied.

GARCIA could not let it rest there. He asked her, "Doctor, you are not telling this jury that's the only way these bruises could have gotten on those legs, by trying to open the legs?"

"Right, just by, as you said, grabbing at her legs, grabbing at the knee area, grabbing at the thighs."

"Thank you, Doctor," Garcia concluded.

SELLS' confessions had been read in court and the video-tape of his walk-through of the crime scene had been viewed. The submission of these documents into evidence compelled Garcia to recall Larry Pope to the stand.

He asked him, "Now, then, you come along sometime in the afternoon and you need another confession, right?"

"[. . .] I had a question about a statement that was made in the first confession, and I wanted to clear it up," Pope responded.

"Actually, Mr. Pope, I believe the truth would be that in this confession that you had with him before, you knew that you could not make a capital murder case, and that's the truth, isn't it?"

"Mr. Garcia, the truth is what I have been telling you."

"Isn't it true that when you went back, the confession number three, you still did not have the answer that you wanted, that there was, in fact, a sexual assault, and that's what you needed?"

Pope bristled. "I did not need sexual assault. I didn't need a capital murder case. I didn't even need trespassing on this man. If the facts dictated that was the charge, then that would be the facts. You have read that statement and it speaks for itself, I believe, on saying about the capital murder charge."

"[. . .] Were you not thinking at that time that you were having trouble making capital murder?"

"I'm not trying to make capital murder. I'm trying to just make what the facts tell me. If you are asking me, 'Did I think there was a capital murder charge there?' there had been a warrant issued for capital murder. I wasn't sure if it was a capital murder charge, but I'm far from being an attorney."

"I understand you," Garcia soothed. "Do you remember when we had a prior proceeding?"

"Yes, sir."

"Do you remember that—it was one of your answers— that you said at this time, 'I thought we were having trouble making capital murder in my mind, because I thought that if he gave me this statement he would end up standing trial for capital murder'?"

"After he gave me the statement, I thought he would end up standing trial for capital murder. I just told you, sir, that I did not think in my mind that this was going to be capital murder prior to this statement."

"So it was not until you got State Exhibit Number Five, which, by the way, is the last one you got?"

"Yes, sir."

"When you finally got him to tell you that he had some penetration?"

"He did say he had penetration in this statement. The facts, all along, indicated that there has been something sexual tied to this murder."

"But," Garcia insisted, "you needed confession number three?"

"I got that. I don't know if I would say I 'needed' anything."

"You told Tommy Sells that if he would admit penetration that he would more than likely be getting the death penalty?"

"No way in the world [. . .]. There is no deal made between me and Tommy Sells about the death penalty."

"Did you inform him prior to the time that he signed the confession number three that with that certain admission he would, in fact, be getting the death penalty, yes or no?"

"In that statement, as it says, he was brought in and he was asked a question. He answered the question that he had penetrated the girl. I informed him that I could not use [. . .] his verbal statement against him in court, that if that was the truth, I would like for him to give me a written statement saying that. But I needed to warn him that if he gave me a written statement saying that, he would be charged with a capital offense and could be given the death penalty. I think I even said, 'would be given the death penalty,' because I wanted to make sure he knew how serious this was."

Garcia continued to press Pope. "Tommy Sells was telling you during this whole time from January second that he wanted to die."

"January second, Tommy Sells told us he did not want to spend the rest of his life in prison. He wanted to die."

"You knew that?" Garcia asked.

"I knew he said that."

"And you had conversations with him all the way up to January seventh when you knew Tommy Sells would do whatever he could because he wanted to die?"

"No, sir, he had quit saying that. On January second when he said that, we talked to him, told him he would be changing his mind on that deal. When he was initially brought in, he was upset, I guess, and I think—I have heard talk before from people first arrested."

ON re-direct, Pope told Hernandez, "I called him into my room, told him there was [. . .] one of the statements he had made that I really didn't understand what he was telling me [. . .] I asked him if he could tell me what that meant."

Hernandez led Pope to clarification of the death wish expressed by Sells. Pope said, "When we first arrested him, when we first brought him in, he said he didn't want to spend the rest of his life in prison. He was upset. He said he had just as soon die. He would rather die than spend the rest of his life in prison. He said that to me at least twice, I would say, that morning."

"Have you heard that before from other defendants?" Hernandez asked.

"Yes, I have heard that from people arrested for a lot smaller things than this."

ON re-cross, Defense Attorney Garcia scored a point by leaving a question hanging in the air: "If this man is a danger to society, then why was he allowed to make a crime-scene walk-through without handcuffs, leg irons or not being held by the arm?"

CHAPTER THIRTY-THREE

On the final day of testimony, Deputy Larry Stamps took the stand. He testified about retrieving Sells' clothing from the laundry basket in his home, his trip to Val Verde Medical Center to photograph Krystal Surles before she was airlifted to San Antonio and other areas of his involvement in the case. According to Lieutenant Pope, Stamps had glorified his own role in the investigation from the beginning. Pope said Stamps had never been the pivotal figure he wanted everyone to think he was. Sells did not care much for him either. He wrote, "Bobby said I need to keep my cool. Stamps is lying his ass off."

Defense Attorney Victor Garcia had no questions for this witness on cross-examination.

Stamps was followed by Dr. Cynthia Beamer, the physician who treated Krystal Surles on the ninth floor of the Janie Brisco Unit at the University of Texas Health Science Center, University Hospital, in San Antonio. She explained how Krystal's injuries had brought her close to death that night from three different causes related to the incision of her neck.

The fact that she was even testifying elicited this angry written retort from Sells: "Bull shit! I've done pled guilty."

Dr. Beamer said, "When I received her into my care, she had a tracheotomy, which is basically a tube that bypasses the voice box and goes into the trachea and allowed her to breathe off a ventilator."

"Explain to us what type of wound it was," asked the State.

"The wound that she sustained is normally a lethal

wound. [. . .] Your voice box or larynx sits on top of your windpipe or trachea. If you feel for your Adam's apple [. . .], the injury was just above the Adam's apple, angling down, coming and getting the arytenoid, which is the cartilage that holds on to your vocal cords, so it angled back and down, and it got into the sheath that surrounds both the carotid artery and the internal jugular."

After further description of her injuries, Hernandez asked the doctor, "Now, you mentioned that the wound, I believe, severed the sheath around the carotid artery?"

"That is correct, sir."

"What would have happened if the carotid artery had been severed?"

"The carotid is the major artery to your head. Had that been severed, she would have died within a matter of minutes."

Then, Hernandez questioned her about the second potentially fatal wound. "Was the trachea severed as well?"

"It did mention in the operative report that the trachea was indeed severed."

"And with the trachea severed, is a person able to breathe through their mouth and through their nose normally like everyone else would?"

"No," Dr. Beamer responded, "and she had so much swelling, too, that she was probably just breathing through her neck at that time almost as if it were a man-made tracheostomy."

"So she would have been breathing through that hole?"

"Through the hole."

"Through the gaping hole?" Hernandez asked in a tone that indicated he could not believe it was possible. "Was there any significance to the swelling? What would that do?"

"Well, it is actually very remarkable that they were able to intubate her in Del Rio prior to sending her to San Antonio. There was so much swelling and distortion of the anatomy [. . .] it is amazing they got an airway. The swelling would have caused her to suffocate slowly. She would not be able to breathe."

Finally, the testimony focused on the third complication that could have, in and of itself, caused Krystal's death. "Now, we have seen that the wound is pretty big. Was there any possibility of blood seeping into the lungs or anything like that?" Hernandez asked.

"Yes, sir. It was a five-inch cut across her neck, and there are many vessels in that area besides just the carotid and the internal jugular. The blood itself could drain into her lungs and basically she could have drowned in her own blood."

When Dr. Beamer stepped down, Sells wrote to Gonzales, "Bobby had no questions after state passed her. This doctor really made me look bad. I just cannot understand why Bobby won't put up a fight on the last two."

Dr. Beamer was followed by a series of experts who testified about the handling, the analysis and the results of their investigation into DNA, blood and fiber evidence.

Sells was confused about the technical explanations about the DNA. He complained to his attorney about what he did not understand. He added, "Going way over my head."

Later during this same group of witnesses, he wrote to Gonzales, "No fight in Bobby."

On the morning of Thursday, September 14, after just three days of testimony, the prosecution announced completion of its presentation. The jury retired from the courtroom as the defense made a request for an instructed verdict of not guilty on the capital murder charge.

Garcia cited the legal need for independent evidence showing that the crime in a confession actually was committed. He argued that the State had not presented any evidence to demonstrate aggravated sexual assault. The State argued that, although their expert could not testify that a sexual assault was a fact, her testimony—and the statements of others—was consistent with sexual assault.

When the request of the defense was denied, the jurors

returned to the courtroom. The defense did not call any witnesses. They simply rested their case. Closing arguments were scheduled for the next Monday, September 18.

FRED Hernandez threaded his arguments in and out of a summation of instructions to the jury. He addressed the jury with passionate eyes, hard-hitting words and an erect posture. "I want you to remember this throughout your deliberations. Actions speak louder than words. We have all heard that phrase before. People can say one thing and, with their actions, mean, do and intend something totally different—and that is what this case is about. This case comes down to: What did the defendant, Tommy Lynn Sells, intend to do the night of December thirtieth of 1999, going into the early morning hours of December thirty-first, 1999."

Sells scribbled on his legal pad, "If the truth was in Fred, he would fall over."

"We listened to his confessions. You saw the videos. Actually, you saw two videos, and then you saw two written statements as well. Pay attention to what he says and how he says it in there. [. . .] you have a written statement, State's Exhibit Four and Five [. . .] and they contain details. However, they cannot convey to you how you say it, how the words are flowing, what his emotions were as he provided the information. But I tell you what," he held a videocassette in the air, "when I played this video for you where he confessed, you got to see what Tommy Lynn Sells was really about, because then you got to hear it in his own words, how he sat there so calm, so cool, so calculating, with callous indifference. You got to see the real Tommy Lynn Sells in that video."

Hernandez summarized the testimony of the witnesses who saw Sells in the hours before the attack. "The defendant knew exactly what he was doing that night. On the video it says, 'I don't think you found my prints. I doubt it. I'm pretty careful about that.' What does that tell you, when somebody goes into a house and is concerned about whether or not they are leaving fingerprints? I walk into this courtroom and leave my fingerprints all over the place. We all do that. We don't even stop to think about that. That isn't something that even enters our mind, but yet it was in his mind."

Sells wrote to his attorney, "I guess what I'm doing is writing just to keep from putting my foot up Fred's ass. This gives me something to do. This would not bother me as bad if Fred was telling the truth."

The prosecutor reviewed the court's instructions to the jury inserting arguments to support the State's charges. "Well, we know that Kaylene Harris was brutally murdered in the early morning hours of December the thirty-first of 1999, because we have an eyewitness. Luckily. Had it not been for that eyewitness, perhaps this case wouldn't have been solved, because remember, there were no fingerprints, no shoeprints, no physical evidence that Tommy Lynn Sells had gone in the Harris residence. Think about how scary that would have been. By millimeters, this case could have been very, very different, because that's all that brave little Krystal Surles survived by, millimeters, because the sheath had already been cut to her carotid. You cut that sheath [sic]—What did Dr. Beamer say? She would have bled in minutes, just like Kaylene. Didn't take Kaylene very long to die. It didn't, and that's how long it would have taken Krystal as well. Lucky. Lucky for her, and for everybody else in our community she survived, because if she doesn't, this is a different ball game."

The state's attorney picked up a photograph of the Harris home. "There is a reason why Tommy Sells went out to the Harris residence, amongst the many. First of all, it is desolate out there. Look at that." He walked the length of the jury box with the picture facing his audience. "I mean, you have to drive to Guajia Bay. It is a quarter mile to the nearest house. I mean, it was an easy target. He had an opportunity because Terry Harris was gone. That calls for some planning."

"Fred is so weak. He is a punk," Sells scratched across the paper.

Hernandez then showed a picture of the living Kaylene Harris to the jury. "This is what she looked like. Pretty little girl. Breathing, smiling. Look at the wind in her hair. She must have been having a good time."

He held up a post-mortem photograph. "This is what Tommy Lynn Sells did with Kaylene Harris. This is what he reduced her to."

Hernandez flashed a series of gruesome photos before the jurors' eyes as he reiterated the magnitude of Kaylene's injuries. "Talk about intent, what do we see?" He waved Kaylene's "Wrap Yourself in Love" shirt in the courtroom. "This is a nightshirt Kaylene Harris was wearing. Look at all the blood. Everywhere, stab wounds, going right to what the defendant intended to do."

He picked up her shorts. "How unusual that the shorts don't seem to have much blood, if any, on them. There might be a stain over here on the front. Those aren't blood-soaked, certainly not like the tee shirt. There is a few specks here. And then the panties." He presents them to the jury with a flourish. "Again, these are not blood-soaked either. You ask yourself, 'Why are the shorts and panties not blood-soaked, but the tee shirt is?' and I'll tell you why. Because he went there with a specific intent to commit this aggravated sexual assault, and he cut them off early in the process. That is what happened.

"[. . .] You can ask yourself why. We're never going to know why he did it, but we are going to know that Kaylene put up a fight. She's a little girl, five-three and one-fourteen. That's not realistically much of a fight she can put up, but the bruises on her legs told you that some-body grabbed her legs [. . .]. Tommy Lynn Sells tried to open Kaylene Harris' legs and she wouldn't. She struggled with him. [. . .] Krystal told you she struggled. Even the defendant admits that the victim struggled. And what sort of signs do we see of a struggle? Well, the doctor said, 'I found what are normally referred to as defensive wounds.'

In other words, wounds where somebody will put up their hands or their arms to keep from getting cut or stabbed. Look at her little hands. Look at the marks on it. She did put up a fight. She did put up her hands. She was trying to keep this man from killing her. Not only her hands, her arms."

He concluded with a plea to the jury. "Horrible, horrible crime, and a man with bad intentions. He went to the Harris house to commit an aggravated sexual assault, and he also tells you that in the video: 'I thought about raping Crystal.' What does he do? He goes to the bedroom where he commits this horrible, horrible crime, and now I ask that you find the defendant, Tommy Lynn Sells, guilty of the offense of capital murder."

AFTER a short recess, Victor Garcia rose to make the argument for the defense. "When Tommy Lynn Sells pled guilty to attempted murder, he accepted responsibility for what he did. Nobody ever asked Tommy Sells in this courtroom if he was guilty of murder, because he is. [. . .] He isn't [. . .] guilty of capital murder.

"[. . .] Be honest with yourself. When you saw that they took a rape kit from Katy Harris, you expected to hear something. When you saw they took a rape kit from Tommy Lynn Sells, I know you expected to hear something, and then they paraded those rape kits around. Every witness they asked, we took a rape kit, we took vaginal swabs from her mouth, from her anal [sic], from her vagina, and what did you hear? Nothing. There was [. . .] no evidence of sexual assault that came from medical evidence, no sperm, no pubic hairs, nothing.

"[. . .] Give me the opportunity to try to show you why there might be reasonable doubt as to what the State is alleging. I cannot compete with the pictures that they are waving. I cannot compete with the knife that they are waving around. I am not trying to justify what Tommy Sells did. I'm not. As a matter of fact, I hate it, too, more than you can imagine."

Garcia pounded on the importance of reasonable doubt. He stressed the permanence of their decision—of their need for factual certainty. "He intentionally killed Katy Harris. He's guilty of murder, okay? Let's not waste time with some of the things that are all so obvious to you and to me and have been all along. We're talking about intent. We're talking about the aggravated assault."

"Bobby's doing the best he can," Sells wrote to Gonzales. "I should of never talked. But I did. I wanted to stop. I wanted to do the right thing. Because I did the right thing, they want to kill me for it. But that's okay. No hard feelings to none of them."

Garcia continued with his argument. "Right off the top, the law tells you—The law tells you very clearly: In order for it to be a capital murder, you have to find that an offense of burglary was in fact committed, and burglary is without the effective consent if he enters the habitation with intent to commit theft or another felony like aggravated sexual assault.

"Opportunity to have a burglary. See, you can't just go into somebody's trailer and say that it is burglary. You have to intend to commit something. [. . .] Lesser charge of murder; he's guilty of murder. You know that. I know that. On the attempted capital murder he pled guilty to you. He told you, 'Yes I did it.' "

Using excerpts from the videotaped confession and walk-through, Garcia, point by point, attacks the credibility of the prosecution's interpretation of the evidence and of Sells' intent.

When he played portions of the original confession, Sells wrote, "Bobby put on the first tape. Breaking me up some more. God, I feel so bad today it's not funny. Head hurts. Cannot breathe right. Chest hurts. Mouth hurts."

Then Garcia showed the jury excerpts from the walk-through tape that supported his contentions. "This tape's killing me even more," Sells scribbled to Gonzales. "I don't understand why Booby [sic] says it will help. This jury is going to kill me. And that's fine by me; I just can't go on with this. My heart's being ripped out every day. And this is like the nail in the coffin."

Garcia questioned the believability of the last confession, the written one. "Tommy Sells is willing to say whatever he can to save himself, and he's telling them, 'Is there anything else that you want? Is there anything else I can do for you?' you know, and then this one is done—they started at ten o'clock at night. There is a question about whether it was a prolonged period of time. Ten o'clock at night, and they end up signing it at almost one o'clock in the morning. Why would they choose that particular time span to do something as important as trying to get a statement, and why wasn't this videotaped? They had the video camera for the other one. They had the video camera to go out to the crime scene. Why not videotape this one?"

Again, Sells defended his attorney in his notes: "Bobby is doing his best with what I gave him to work with. I know I could have walked on this but I wanted to talk. I wanted to die that's why I can be at peace with myself. Whatever way it goes is okay with me."

"But you see," Garcia continued, "that's not enough. It is still not enough. They have to go back and they have got to get State's Exhibit Number Five. They have to. They need it. [. . .] They already told them, 'We don't have capital unless we can prove a sexual assault. The tape isn't any good. State's Exhibit Four is not any good. Go get it. And you talk about somebody CYA, covering your ass. They put everything into the sentence that they wanted in one sentence, and they use the rest of it to try to explain how they didn't coerce him, threaten him or promise him or do anything to get it from him.

"Everything in this statement points to Larry Pope CYA, because they flat-out told Tommy Sells, 'You admit to this, you will get the death penalty.' Tommy Sells had already told them, admitted it, even though it is written on here, he said he wanted to die. Everything that he had done, he says on the tape, it is bad to hurt people, and this is what they got, you can choose to believe Four and Five.

That's your prerogative, but the charge gives you the ability to question whether or not these statements were influenced in any form or fashion, and that benefit should be resolved in favor of the process we have. That's the way that it should be resolved.

"When you get down to it, this is what Tommy confessed to. This is what, later on, they wanted him to tell them, because the physical evidence does not add up, does not add up to their theory of the case. Brutal crime, horrendous as you want to see. I don't like him very much. I don't like him at all, to be honest, and I'm not just saying that, but you have got to consider the evidence for what it is worth."

In response to these words, Sells scrawled on his paper: "This hurt me."

"Tommy Lynn Sells is guilty of murder, by his own words, but he's not guilty of capital murder. There is not sufficient evidence to raise it to the point that you can decide without hesitation that his only intent as he entered the trailer was specifically to commit aggravated sexual assault.

"He goes into the mom's room and he says, 'I don't have a plan.' Then he says, 'You know, I was going to rape her; oh, I'm too drunk.' Well, if he's too drunk to rape the mother, what makes you think he's going to be able to rape, you know, another girl? That's what makes this case so difficult. That's what makes this case take—at least warrant the amount of time to independently consider. What happens to our system when you can go in there and say, 'You know what? that's good enough for me. You know what? Fine. He said he did it. Let's kill him.' Don't do that to yourselves.

"[. . .] Because the State of Texas has the burden of proof [. . .] they get to stand up here again, and Fred Hernandez is going to knock me down like you wouldn't believe. 'Mr. Garcia says this, Mr. Garcia says that.' He's probably going to pound, he's going to wave pictures, he's going to wave the knife at you. He has the right to do that. He has the right to plead for law enforcement, say, 'Let's not let this happen in our county, let's not let murders happen in our county. Let's not let capital murders happen in our county.' Except this doesn't fit under the State's evidence. It doesn't fit. Tough. Tell him to explain to you how that bra got the mark and the scratches on the breast if the bra was already off. Tell him to explain to you how Katy's blood was on those shorts and on the underwear, and so was Krystal's, if he's saying that they were not anywhere close to the crime scene. Tell him to explain to you how Tommy's shirt cannot be soaked in blood also if he was holding her from behind and he cut her neck from behind [. . .] You have to find one of the hardest things to prove, and that is somebody's intent, and actions, ladies and gentlemen, speak louder than words.

"[. . .] You have a very difficult job ahead of you. I don't envy you. Take it serious. Take your time. Consider it, and maybe you might even go one step further, say. You know what? After Mr. Hernandez sits down, think of what I would have said if I had been given an opportunity to get back up here again. I don't condone, you don't condone, the system doesn't condone what Tommy Lynn Sells did. You never will, but this is not a capital murder case. He's guilty of murder; he's not guilty of capital murder."

FRED Hernandez faced the jury and responded to each point of doubt raised by the defense. Then he said, "Let's talk about intent, what this case really turns on, intent. Now, what kind of person is going to go wander aimlessly into somebody's house with a knife? 'I just happened to have a big old knife. [. . .] I'm just going to carry that into some stranger's house.' Right. Of course not. He knew exactly what he was doing. [. . .] He surveys the entire house, finds out it is just the women and the little blind boy. Boom, he's got an opportunity and he takes it. This is an opportunist.

"His story is, 'I just spontaneously went,' or this thing about cocaine. Give me a break. [. . .] That's not the reason he went over there. He went over there to commit aggravated sexual assault, whether it was against Katy Harris or whether it was against Crystal Harris. [. . .] Remember what the court told you: Penetration, no matter how slight. And the burden of proof has been met. We didn't need to have this massive trauma to show that. That's extra. All I have to show you is that he intended to do that when he went over there, and the evidence is clear on that."

"[. . .] Next week, September twenty-seventh, Katy would have been fourteen years old." He held the picture of the lively young teen before the jury. "Look at that smile. She didn't get to be fourteen or fifteen or eighteen. There will be no high school graduation, no prom, no college, no marriage, no kids, and all because the defendant, Tommy Lynn Sells, went over there and he took her life in the most brutal, horrible fashion we can imagine."

Sells wrote to Gonzales, "I can't put the pen down. If I do I would jump on Fred. The truth is not in him. Blowing smoke. Smoke only."

Fred Hernandez continued, "He says in his confession, 'I'm not telling you this to get a guilty conscience off my mind.' He didn't care. There wasn't a shred of guilt in him. He's just talking like it's an everyday, ordinary occurrence. [. . .] He knew exactly what he was doing before he got there, when he got there and after he left.

"Cases like this are always very hard, but I want you to think back to something Crystal Harris said. She said, 'I didn't know what had happened in my home. I saw the ambulance at the Betzes', and I saw the ambulance at my house, and I saw them take somebody out of the Betzes' residence, and the ambulance left. And then she said, 'I then saw the ambulance at my house leave with no body,' and she said, 'I knew somebody hadn't made it,' and she was worried because she had been in charge of two other children that didn't belong to her. She was worried about them, and she's trying to figure out who is left over that has not been accounted for, so she starts asking questions, and by asking the age of the child that was taken in the ambulance, she said at that point in time, 'I knew my Katy hadn't made it,' and she said, 'I sat there and I cried and I cried.' Can you imagine the pain of the mother, knowing that she was never going to see her daughter again that horrible morning? That is what this case is about, and I ask you to find the defendant, Tommy Lynn Sells, guilty of capital murder."

AFTER two short hours of deliberation, the jury returned. They found Tommy Lynn Sells guilty on all three charges, one count of attempted murder and two counts of capital murder.

CHAPTER THIRTY-FOUR

THE next day, the punishment phase of the trial began. In it, the jury had to answer two special issue questions. First: "Is there a probability that the defendant, Tommy Lynn Sells, would commit criminal acts of violence that would constitute a continuing threat to society?" Then they must answer the second question: "Taking into consideration all of the evidence, including the circumstances of the offense, the defendant's character and background, and the personal moral culpability of the defendant, do you find there is sufficient mitigating circumstance or circumstances to warrant that a sentence of life imprisonment rather than the death sentence should be imposed?"

To bolster its claim that the death penalty was called for in this case, the prosecution called a series of witnesses. Danny Calderon, a prisoner in the Val Verde County Jail, testified that Sells had threatened him with a slow death.

Dr. Fredrick Miers stated that, in his opinion, Tommy Lynn Sells was an anti-social personality. Individuals with anti-social personality disorder demonstrate a lack of concern for others, an absence of shamefulness and guilt and a disregard for society's expectations and laws. They are irritable and aggressive, good at manipulating others and highly impulsive. They posses a pervasive disregard for other people, and cannot or will not conform to the norms of society. Their lives are characterized by frequent imprisonment for unlawful behavior, alcoholism and drug abuse. Homicide or suicide is common. There is no known effective treatment for people with anti-social personality disorder.

Dr. Miers believed there was a strong probability that Sells would commit criminal acts of violence and would constitute a continuing threat to society. To strengthen the doctor's opinion, Hernandez went back over his testimony and asked him targeted questions. He inquired about an incident that had occurred on June 9, 2000, at the Terrel Unit of the Texas prison system. A death row in mate assaulted a 78-year-old prison chaplain. He grabbed the chaplain's arm into his cell, tied it with a sheet and cut on him with razor blades at the end of a shank.

"You are familiar with the chaplain that was recently attacked and stabbed in the penitentiary [. . .]"

"Yes."

"In fact, that attack took place by a defendant that was on death row, is that correct?"

"[. . .] On that attack, that was my understanding," the doctor agreed.

"And he almost severed his hand with that razor?"

"It was a very serious injury."

"The point I'm making is that if Tommy Lynn Sells wants a weapon, he can get it in prison."

"Yes, he can."

"And of course, you testified that both drugs and alcohol are available in the penitentiary as well."

"Yes."

"Then you talked about motivation. Are you telling us that Tommy Lynn Sells is not going to have any type of conflict in prison?"

"I am certainly not," Doctor Miers replied. "All I'm telling you is that the range and nature of that conflict will be—and potential targets coming out of that will be—seriously circumscribed."

"If he's in the general population, there is not a potential for conflict?"

"Yes, there is, but . . ."

Hernandez interrupted. "In fact, for him it is probably pretty high?"

"Perhaps."

"Because of the nature of the offense."

"Oh yeah. Oh yeah."

"Then you talk about intent. The fact of the matter is, if somebody wants to stab somebody or slash somebody or kill somebody in the penitentiary, if they are intent on doing it, they are going to do it."

"If they really make up their mind, they are going to do it unless restrained."

"Now, do prisoners ever escape from the penitentiary?" From the look on Hernandez's face, it was obvious he'd looked forward to asking this question. He eagerly waited for the answer he knew he would get.

"Occasionally."

"In fact, they even escape from death row."

"Yes."

THE State next called Royce Smithey, chief investigator for the Special Prison Unit. His job responsibility was the investigation and prosecution of felony offenses that occur inside the prison system.

District Attorney Thomas F. Lee questioned him about the likeliness of violence in prisons, then asked him, "So if, in other words, if an individual goes into prison and his mind is set on doing violent acts, there is no way you can stop that?"

"No, sir," he answered, "there is no way."

VICTOR Garcia stepped forward for cross-examination. "Mr. Smithey, how many inmates does the Texas prison system hold?"

"Do they hold now?"

"Yes."

"Approximately one hundred fifty thousand."

"So you are telling this jury that you handle one hundred fifty thousand complaints every year?"

"No, sir." His answer snapped back like a sneer.

"You have led this jury to believe that in the prison system, [. . .] your unit is involved on a daily basis because every inmate in that prison is violent and every inmate in that prison system does some sort of violent act, every inmate in that prison system has a knife . . ."

Garcia was interrupted by an objection from District Attorney Lee. Once it was overruled, the defense continued, "Is that what you are telling this jury?"

"No, sir. No, sir."

"The last question Mr. Lee asked you, if a person, if an inmate has an intense desire to commit an act, he can do it."

"Yes, sir," Smithey agreed.

"If an inmate does not have an intent to do the act, then he won't."

"Correct."

"And the majority of inmates that are in the prison system don't do violent acts."

"That's correct."

"As a matter of fact," Garcia continued, "there is a very small percentage of the hundred and fifty thousand that actually do commit criminal acts of violence?"

"Yes, sir, that's correct."

"Sometimes it is the same inmate that does multiple ones."

"That's correct."

"Are you also telling us that the prison system that you said is not working . . ."

Smithey cut him off. "I don't believe I said it wasn't working. I said I believe it works probably better than any other system in the United States, maybe in the world."

"Okay. I believe your last answer to his question was that the current prison system is not working?"

"I don't believe I answered that question. No, sir. I don't believe that question was asked. I think the last question was asked, 'If a person wants to be violent they can be violent' and my response was, 'Yes, they can.' "

"No, let me ask it again, then. You were talking about a prison system that is not very effective [. . .] keeping acts of violence from occurring within the prison system."

"Well, first part of your question, no, I'm not talking about a system that doesn't work. The system does work. It works as well as humanly possible. The Texas prison system is by far the best system in the United States when it comes to violence. [...] The second part of your question is, basically, if a person wants to be violent, they can be violent, and there is nothing that this prison system, or any other prison system in the United States, can do under the way that they are allowed to operate. There are things that you can do to guarantee a person won't be violent, but some of those are illegal, and other ways—go ahead." Smithey paused, concerned that he was about to step on forbidden ground. He looked over to the district attorney, then to the judge and back to the defense attorney. "You probably—You want me to go ahead and answer?"

"Go ahead and answer," Garcia responded.

"If you guarantee a person won't be violent, you put them on death row and execute them, and I guarantee they won't be violent after that."

HERB Betz had one more role to play in this phase of the trial. He had been asked to read a statement written by Krystal's father, Mark. Her father could not be in the courtroom because he was hundreds of miles away, serving time in jail on a marijuana charge.

Herb thought he was ready to read this statement. He'd been watching Sells throughout the trial. He saw him writing, drawing, jiggling his leg, and always with that smirky grin that never seemed to leave his face. That grin filled Herb with righteous indignation—enough, he thought, to read this statement without an emotional display.

"This is, by far, the most difficult statement I have ever given, but it is the most urgent and heartfelt." As Herb read on, he felt the lump building in his throat.

"Though I choose to follow what Jesus Christ would do, and that is to forgive you, Tommy Lynn Sells, this does not change the fact that we must reap what we sow. The depth of the losses you have brought into our lives with your own hands cannot and will not be accepted or tolerated. The senseless brutal sexual assault and murder of the little girl, Kaylene Harris, and the attempted murder of my daughter, Krystal Surles, is nothing short of evil." Herb blinked and swallowed hard, taking a sip of water before he continued.

"Taking lives away from families to satisfy your own lust is a disgrace to mankind, America and the State of Texas, not to mention God. Maybe the court and you, Tommy Lynn Sells, will never know how much Krystal's and our lives have changed, i.e., the memories of Krystal's friend dying at your hands, the nightmares and physical scars that may never heal. Yes, your run of terror has changed lives forever.

"As a father and a man who knows our judicial system, first-hand, I am asking this court and the ones who represent these two little girls, their families and all of us who will never tolerate such acts of violence, that you, Tommy Sells, be given the death penalty. And that from this time forth, no one else will ever suffer at your hands again. May God have mercy on your soul. Mark Surles."

Then Herb read the note at the bottom that Mark had addressed to his daughter. Before he opened his mouth, the tears began to flow. "To you, Krystal, you are the most precious, honest, loving, brave and toughest little girl in the world. The Lord, our Lord, has a special plan for you. I am also the proudest father ever. I love you, baby, your Dad."

A shaken Herb Betz took his seat as he relived the pain and wonder of the first day he met Krystal Surles.

THE defense called Dr. Wendell Lee Dickerson, a psychologist who once worked in a prison system and now works there on an occasional contract basis. Before the trial, Dr. Dickerson had administered an electroencephalogram or EEG, a test that measures brain waves.

Garcia asked, "What did you find after you ran your EEG?"

"[. . .] We did find evidence that there are a fairly large number of abnormalities in his scan."

"What do those abnormalities tell you about Tommy Lynn Sells?"

"Well, that there are abnormalities. They [. . .] can further tell you something about what the nature of those abnormalities are. He has a fairly high frequency of what are called phase and symmetry problems in his EEG. There [. . .] is some evidence that the communication between the front part of his activity in his head and the rear part of the activity don't work very well together. [. . .] This tells you something about his capacity to regulate himself and to inhibit and guide his own conduct."

Dr. Dickerson discussed the high fever Sells and his twin sister experienced that resulted in the girl's death, his "very long and very bad substance abuse history" and the pedophile who had abused him.

Garcia knew his client's only hope for life rested in this man's hands. He continued his questioning. "Now, the information that you have now put together, of all the testing you have done, did that lead you to be able to put some sort of label on what you believe [are] the problems that Tommy Lynn Sells has now?"

"Yes, sir."

"And what would that be?"

"Well, my diagnostic preference, Mr. Garcia, is, he's a borderline personality disorder with schizoid, avoidant and anti-social features, probable brain damage." People with borderline personality disorder can maintain a warm, friendly and competent façade until their social defenses break down in stressful situations. But, essentially, they are unstable individuals. Moods can shift from depression to elation to anger in minutes. Their self-image jumps from elevated to devalued. Relationships with others are stormy— one day a person is an admired friend, the next a despised enemy. They are prone to demonstrate self-damaging behavior such as burning or cutting themselves or even attempting suicide. Treatment of this disorder includes individual psychotherapy and group therapy as well as the use of pharmaceuticals—anti-depressants, anti-psychotics and mood stabilizers. Many improve with proper psychiatric care and are able to lead productive lives.

When Garcia pointed out that Dr. Miers had testified that Sells had anti-social personality disorder, Dr. Dickerson said, "I think, Mr. Garcia, that's a fairly common mistake that is made at the courthouse. We encounter individuals all the time with criminal history of some length or another, and the first thing that pops into everybody's mind is, 'We're dealing with an anti-social personality disorder.' "

Now, Garcia asked an important question for the defense. "If Tommy Lynn Sells is removed from the opportunity, Tommy Lynn Sells is medicated, he would not carry out some of these disorders that you have found?" Then he waited for a response that would force the jurors to answer "yes" to special issue question number one, regarding the likelihood of continued acts of violence.

"I think, you know, if you remove him and medicate him, then you have changed the risk factors. Medication serves to raise the barrier. It serves to raise his capacity to inhibit these things. You are not going to make some of the stuff that is buried in him go away, but it [. . .] can improve his capacity for self-management, and I might say that the longer he stays drug-free, the better chance he's got of making some improvement. Street drug–free."

Wanting to embed this assessment in the minds of every juror, Garcia touched on the issue again. "You yourself have worked within the prison system, correct?"

"Yes."

"You have seen how inmates are controlled?"

"Yes."

"And you feel that if Tommy Lynn Sells was in that controlled environment in a penitentiary system, that that would, in your opinion, eliminate the risk of Tommy Lynn Sells committing acts of violence in the future?"

"Mr. Garcia, I have a great deal of confidence in our

penitentiary system. I think they can handle anybody."

"[. . .] Is there a probability that Tommy Lynn Sells would commit criminal acts of violence and be a continuing threat to society, based on the information you have?"

"In or out of the penitentiary?"

"In the penitentiary."

"Mr. Garcia, I'm not going to split some hairs with you on this one. I think Tommy Lynn Sells is probably going to be much more of a target than he is an instigator of trouble if he is in the general population. They are going to have to protect him."

On summation, Fred Hernandez first reviewed the instructions to the jurors. Then he proceeded with his argument. "Brutal, sadistic, cold-blooded crime. There is no other way to describe it. There is absolutely no other way to describe it. I told you it was gruesome, but it is really beyond that. Is this how anybody wants to end up dying? Is this how we want our children to end up dying?

"There are lots of photographs." He displayed the autopsy photographs one by one as he talked to the jurors. "They are all horrible. Is this where we want our children to end up, on a cold slab as a forensic pathologist looks at the wounds, front and back? And just look at the nature of the wounds all over her little body, from the neck down to her legs."

He ticked off a capsule summary of the points of evidence the prosecution had presented in the penalty phase. "Dr. Miers went on to talk about the videotapes and how they struck him, because there was such a lack of emotion, and you saw the tapes, and if you want to play them again when you go back to the jury room, take them with you and play them. He was so cavalier about it that it was like going to the grocery store and picking up fruit. That is how the defendant, Tommy Lynn Sells, looked in those two videos, that he showed a total lack of remorse. That goes along with what Dr. Dickerson thought in the MMPI [. . .] that he didn't have any empathy means he doesn't have any feelings toward anybody else. He doesn't care. He could care less."

Often Hernandez referred back to evidence revealed in the guilt–innocence portion of the trial. He argued, "Now, we have all heard the term, you know, 'Trouble follows some people around.' Do you know what? Trouble doesn't follow Tommy Sells around. He is the trouble. Where he goes, he takes trouble with him.

"And regardless of what you want to call him, whether you want to call him an anti-social person or a borderline personality disorder person, Dr. Dickerson said he's a 'very alarming person.' Those were his exact words, 'very alarming person.' That's a nice way for saying he's a scary guy. That's what that means."

In conclusion, the assistant D.A. insisted, "There is no doubt that Tommy Lynn Sells will continue to be a threat to society in general, whether it be to us or in the penitentiary. The only thing that is left for you to decide is whether or not there is a sufficient mitigating circumstance to warrant you giving him a life sentence as opposed to a death sentence. You know what? He gave Katy a death sentence. Next Wednesday would have been Katy's birthday. She would have been fourteen. No more. No high school graduation. No first day of college. No wedding day jitters. No first children. No grandchildren. It is your job and duty to send a message to Tommy Lynn Sells, and to tell him that what he did was beyond horrendous, beyond brutal, beyond sadistic. Tell him that whatever pleasure he derived from killing Katy Harris, for that, in and of itself, he must forfeit his life.

"Answer special issue number one with a yes, that he will be a future danger, and answer number two no, that there is no mitigating factor that will warrant him receiving a life sentence. Don't do it only for Katy Harris. Do it for all of the people and children of our community. Send a message to Tommy Lynn Sells that we will not tolerate, absolutely not tolerate this type of behavior in our community."

THIS moment weighed very heavily on Victor Roberto Garcia. It was his last opportunity to save the life of his client. He rose slowly and faced the jury. First, he reminded them of the promise they had made to "[. . .] not be swayed by sentiment, conjecture, sympathy, passion, prejudice, public opinion or feeling.

"[. . .] Mr. Hernandez just spent twenty minutes of the forty minutes that he took talking to you about emotion, talking to you about photographs, because that's what he wants you to do, to ignore the evidence that is before you, look at Katy's picture, look at Krystal and say, 'You are going to die; we're going to kill you, Tommy Lynn Sells, and that's all there is to it.' That's not what the law says."

Garcia went on to address the issue of mitigating circumstances. "It doesn't justify what Tommy Lynn Sells did, but for the last twenty years he has been a victim of our own society, somebody's own choosing. He chose to take drugs on his own. I'm not setting that aside, but as very young man, he was victimized by child abuse. [. . .] By the age of thirteen years old, he was already in a state hospital where they diagnosed him. They have known the problem exists. Dr. Dickerson told you, and Dr. Miers did not contradict it. Tommy Lynn Sells has a lot of problems."

The defense attorney moved on, comparing the two psychiatrists. "When you consider Dr. Dickerson and you consider Dr. Miers' testimony, you have to weigh them. Dr. Miers looked at these photographs, read the reports, saw the video confession and said, 'This man needs to be killed. That's the only way we can control him. There is no other way.'

"[. . .] That's not what Dr. Dickerson did. Call it antisocial, call it borderline, it doesn't make any difference. Tommy Lynn Sells has a lot of problems. Do you have to kill Tommy Lynn Sells to control him?

"You know, I was kind of irate at Smithey, who testified because he seemed to be wanting you to believe that every inmate in the prison system can get a knife, that every inmate in the prison system has whatever drugs they want, and that every inmate commits some sort of act of violence. If that's true, shut the court down, send the word to the prison system and say, 'Kill one hundred and fifty thousand inmates, because there is a likelihood, since they are in prison, that they are going to get a knife, that they are going to get drugs, and that they are going to hurt somebody. Let's just kill one hundred and fifty thousand people and get rid of the problem.'

"You say, 'Well, let's just kill Tommy Sells. That will take care of his problem.' See, but that's where Dr. Dickerson comes in and tells you when a person [. . .] serves a life in prison, they can treat what they know he has. He has some brain dysfunction that can be treated. He has some disorders that can be treated."

Garcia argued for the life of his client. "When he came in to you and pled guilty to Krystal Surles, that has to mean something to you. He came here on his confession and said, 'I killed Katy Harris.' That has to mean something. We're talking about justice. [. . .] Justice requires that you follow the law that the State of Texas has given you. If you decide that Tommy Lynn Sells should live, and it is in your hands, every day that Tommy Lynn Sells sees the sun go up, he's going to be incarcerated. Every day for the rest of his life that he sees the sun go down, he's going to be incarcerated. Mr. Hernandez is going to go back and tell you Katy doesn't have that opportunity, and that's true; she doesn't. But make him think about it for every day for the rest of his life, think about what he did to Katy Harris every single day. When you think about it, if Tommy Lynn Sells lives to be seventy years old, seventy years old, he's going to be sitting in his cell and he's going to look at a calendar and say, 'You know what? I still have five more years before I can even be considered, before they will even look.' At seventy years old, he's still going to be sitting in his cell every day.

"[. . .] You cannot decide this case on emotion. You

cannot decide this case just on sympathy, passion, prejudice or public opinion. You should not decide this case because Terry and Crystal Harris are crying, because they are hollering, and they are going to for a long time. Nothing justifies what Tommy Lynn Sells did. But has it been proven to you that he's going to commit criminal acts of violence in the future? Can you tell me, is there anything that mitigates this case? That's something that only you can decide. Only you can decide, and I'll submit to you that the last nine months are an indication. The fact that, thank God, that Krystal Surles is still here, thank God for that. I can only tell you, don't decide this case on vengeance. 'Vengeance is mine,' says the Lord."

In his rebuttal, Hernandez begged for death as intently as any one victim of Tommy Lynn Sells ever pleaded for life. "Nobody has enjoyed going through this case. It was horrible. Very difficult, very emotional for everybody in it, starting with the family, on down to the lawyers. It takes a lot out of everybody, including you. I'm sure that nobody in this courtroom wants to be here.

"The last person that wants to be here is Tommy Lynn Sells, and that's why he took the screens from the house, and said, 'I didn't leave any prints. I doubt if you will find any.' He didn't expect to be here. He didn't expect to be here because he thought he had also killed Krystal Surles. When he walked out, he said in this confession, 'I thought she was dead.' I mean, as far as he was concerned, when he walked out of that bedroom in the Harris residence, in his own words, 'I already dropped one; I went back to get the other one.' He just assumed he killed everybody.

"[. . .] This case has really been about actions speaking louder than words, because all you have to do is look at what the defendant has done in the past, track him, look at his convictions and what he's done, how he's escalated, look at where he left Katy, look how he did it.

"[. . .] So what do we do with Tommy Lynn Sells? [. . .] 'How do we insure or guarantee that he won't com-

mit any further criminal acts of violence?' Mr. Garcia asked
Royce Smithey. [. . .] He said the way to do it is to execute
him. I guarantee you he won't commit any further acts of
violence. That's the only way. That's the only way that he
could guarantee that.

"What could justify what this defendant did to Katy?
You have a beautiful little girl. What in the world can justify what he did to her? Can you think of something? Can
you think of a mitigating circumstance that will justify this?
Because if you do, then you tell everybody else what that
circumstance was, because I don't see it. This case is tough,
and we told you about it, and everybody said that they
could follow the law and I'm going to ask you to do that.
Do the right thing and sentence Tommy Lynn Sells to
death."

Now, all that remained was the decision of the jury. No
one had to wait long. After three hours, the jury had finished their deliberations. As they entered the courtroom,
Pam and Krystal Surles and Marlene and Herb Betz took
seats in the front row. They held hands, held their breaths,
held out hope for the death penalty. The jurors presented
their answers to the two special issue questions. "Yes," they
said, Tommy Lynn Sells is a future danger to society. "No,"
they answered, there are no mitigating circumstances in this
case.

For the paltry handful of people in the courtroom who
cared about Tommy Lynn Sells, or objected to the death
penalty on principle, it was a devastating blow. Their sad,
defeated faces and mouths devoid of words were in sharp
contrast to the majority of the courtroom. For the families
and the prosecutors—and for much of the community—it
was a cause for celebration. A moment for lengthy jubilant
interviews—a time to declare that justice had been done.

"We had a lot of volunteers at the courtroom who said
they'd be glad to put the needle in his arm—a lot of people," said Herb Betz.

His wife, Marlene, added, "Most of them just wanted to take him down to the town square.

"Let them stone him to death.

"Let the people take care of him," Marlene concluded.

CHAPTER THIRTY-FIVE

ON November 8, 2000, Tommy Lynn Sells took up residence on death row in the Polunsky Unit in Livingston, Texas. He was given Texas Department of Justice number 999367. He found the restrictions and housing here far more confining than his time in the Val Verde Corrections Center. There was no television to watch. No telephone calls allowed. And smoking was prohibited.

He was housed in a section of a pod containing fourteen prisoners in all, and had to spend twenty-three hours of every day in his cell. It was a six-foot-wide space and contained a sink, a toilet and a bed. Sometimes he slept on the floor, using his bed as a makeshift desk for writing and drawing.

Sells became part of a small death row protest. "Last night on C-pod, we refused to eat supper. Every time Texas kills someone we are going to refuse to eat that last meal of the day and between 6 and 7, there will be silence, no talking. Of 84 cells on C pod, only seven people got a tray. It's respect for the fallen."

He was allowed a shower every three days. Before he could leave his cell, he had to put his hands behind his back and stick them through the bean hole, where a guard slapped on cuffs. The shower was a room seven feet by two feet. After stepping inside, he stuck his hands into the bean hole again and the guard released the cuffs. On a good day, the guard returned to take him back to his cell in ten or fifteen minutes. On a bad day, Sells had to wait in there as much as an hour.

He quickly adapted to the community of men living on

borrowed time. "I cannot stress this enough. In here is home. No matter what I could say, think or do, I could not, cannot make it in your world. When I first started doing time years ago, my outlook was, 'I'm just not getting a foothold on things.' But the older I get, the more I understand that your society changes the rules by not looking out for me as a child, then I see they change the rules again when I get older. Society's rule is day-to-day, person-to-person. Well, prison society, you may become friends with a guard or two over time, and get a few extra things [. . .] but on the whole, my world stays the same. I'm not fighting for my life, get that straight, but I do want the record straight. My life was over a long time ago. I'm living on borrowed time I was born in 1964 and died in 1964."

There were lockdowns in the facility two or three times a year or more. Guards went cell to cell shaking the place down in search of contraband. Even Scotch tape was contraband here—a roll was sold on the black market for twenty postage stamps. During this time, whether it lasted two days or two weeks, Sells and the other prisoners stayed in their quarters round the clock, subsisting on "johnnies," rolled pancakes filled with peanut butter.

Two activities occupied Sells' time: creating artwork from the limited selection of supplies available at the commissary, and maintaining an extensive written correspondence. He heard from a few family members, a couple of prisoners he met in Del Rio, his attorneys, members of the law enforcement community and pen pals he earned with his infamy. These correspondents wrote from every corner of the United States. He even received letters from Europe. It was obvious that some who wrote were disturbed individuals who saw him as an object of admiration or sexual attraction. Others were collectors of serial killer memorabilia. Some were drawn by the same hypnotic fascination that compels passing drivers to stare at the gruesome horror of a fatal car wreck. The Europeans in the group tended to be opposed to the death penalty, and viewed him as the victim of barbaric American justice. He said the only thing that made him feel alive was the mail he received from the outside.

TOMMY Lynn Sells was physically removed from his wife, Jessica. But even in his absence, he created problems for her. Her boys were teased and isolated at school by their peers and teachers alike. She suffered as a powerless witness to their persecution.

She battled to keep her two boys in her home. After rarely visiting them over the last five years, her ex-husband wanted custody. In court, the judge was blunt. She had to stop all communication and visits with Tommy Sells, or the boys would be taken from her.

She ended all contact with her husband. One by one, his family members did the same—only his Aunt Bonnie continued to write with any regularity. "I received a letter last night from Bonnie and she told me Ma Brown died, my grandmother. Just turned the lights out, put in my ear buds, turned up the volume on the radio and closed my eyes. What hurt really bad, I would think my mother or brother would have told me. Life really sucks sometimes."

THE *48 Hours* TV program flew Texas Rangers Johnny Allen and Coy Smith to New York to view the first episode of their two-part series on the crimes of Tommy Lynn Sells. On the morning of February 1, 2001, they appeared on *The Early Show* on CBS. Following a clip of Harold Dow talking to Tommy Lynn Sells, Jane Clayson interviewed the two officers. That night's showing of "Dead Men Tell No Tales" did a better job of alerting the nation's law enforcement agencies than the Rangers had anticipated. When they returned to their offices, they had more than six hundred e-mails and nine hundred phone calls to return.

Again and again, they asked the same questions and got the same answers. "Do you have any fingerprints?"

"No."

"Do you have any DNA evidence?"

"No."

"Do you have any physical evidence to connect a per-petrator to the crime scene?"

"No."

It was apparent that all these crimes were not the work of Tommy Lynn Sells, but the volume of cases was frightening. "It would blow your skirt up over your head if you knew how many serial killers are running around the United States at any one time," said Johnny Allen.

THE same day the *48 Hours* show aired, Susan Reed, district attorney for Bexar County, Texas, took the Mary Bea Perez case to the grand jury in San Antonio. She secured a capital murder indictment against Tommy Lynn Sells.

The documents allege that he choked the 9-year-old girl to death with his hands and then killed her to prevent her from testifying against him.

"It was completely senseless," Reed stated in her press release. "We now have all the evidence we are ever going to get. It is time to get this matter to trial. Even though Mr. Sells has already been sentenced to death, we could not let this chapter in our history remain open."

The indictment was based on Sells' confession, and although items that crime technicians found at the scene were tested, no relevant results were found.

THE night the first "Dead Men Tell No Tales" episode of *48 Hours* aired, the phone rang in Kathleen Cowling's home in Clinton, Mississippi. It was a friend of hers in Memphis who had watched the show and swore that she'd spotted the murderer of Kathleen's first husband, John Cade. She told her that Sells had liked to climb into windows to get into people's homes.

Kathleen assured her friend that she would watch the second part of the show, but thought Sells was an unlikely suspect because he was too young. It may have been more than twenty-one years since the murder of John Cade, but she still thought of him as "the finest man who ever walked the earth." And she yearned for answers about his death.

In preparation for the second episode, she pulled out her copy of a forensic artist's sketch of a suspicious man spotted near her home five hours after John was killed.

A woman visited Grand Gulf State Park with her two children at about 8 o'clock on the morning on July 6, 1979. A young man, who appeared to be high on drugs, frightened all three of them. When he ran toward her, she grabbed her kids, pushed them in the car, and slammed down the door locks. All she wanted was to get out of there, but he got in front of her car and prevented her escape for a short but interminable period of time.

She described him as having a dark complexion, acne scars and short, dark hair. He drove off in a white Chevy with a black interior and Mississippi tags. But most frightening of all was his shirt—it was splattered with blood. A forensic artist worked with her to render a likeness of this unknown man. He was sought as a suspect in John Cade's murder, but was never found.

Kathleen sat down to watch the second episode of "Dead Men Tell No Tales" with the sketch by her side and skepticism in her heart. Soon, the drawing was held in white-knuckled fingers and her heart was in her throat. She compared the man on the screen with the one in the picture in her hand. There were similar curves in the jaw line. The eyebrows of both had the same upward pointed growth in the same places. Sells and the drawing had a distinct line in the chin, an oval-shaped face and wavy hair. And in every photograph flashed on the TV, there were the same tightly closed lips as the ones in the drawing. She'd been begging God for answers to her husband's murder and, at that moment, Tommy Lynn Sells was starting to look like the answer to her prayers.

She wrote to him and asked if he had been in Mississippi in 1979. He wrote back and said in that year he was in Mississippi, Arkansas, Missouri, Tennessee, and maybe California, too.

Her next letter asked if he had had acne when he was 15, if he was driving that summer and if he remembered that July Fourth holiday weekend. He admitted that his face had had severe eruptions at that age, and not only was he driving cars, he was also stealing them. But he could not remember where he was on that particular weekend.

She picked up her pen and wrote again, wanting to know if he remembered any of the cars he had stolen and driven around for a while. And she enclosed a copy of the forensic sketch, asking if he thought that resembled him when he was fifteen. His response mentioned a white Chevrolet that summer.

An intermediary visited Kathleen and told her that Tommy said he had committed that murder in Mississippi. Kathleen was jubilant, but not foolish. She wanted to believe, but first Tommy had to provide her with unpublished details about the crime scene and the events of that night. She wanted to visit Sells with Mississippi lawmen at her side to record and confirm his confession. She did not want any charges filed, she assured him. She only wanted closure.

Sells agreed to talk to her—he agreed to tell her everything—but she could not bring any law enforcement with her. Kathleen's vestigial skepticism was in revival. Without a definitive piece of information, she could not be certain. She didn't want revenge. All she wanted was the truth.

CHAPTER THIRTY-SIX

TOMMY Lynn Sells left death row for the Bexar County Correction Center in San Antonio on February 22, 2001, to await trial there for the capital murder of Mary Bea Perez.

There were those who criticized the district attorney for being politically motivated in her pursuit of the death penalty. Since he was already on death row, the practicality of devoting strained law enforcement resources to this case was questioned. Some thought the expenditure of $200,000–$300,000 for a capital case was a waste of taxpayers' money.

Sells' attorneys made Susan Reed an offer: he would plead guilty in exchange for a life sentence. She consulted with the family of Mary Bea Perez. One half of them wanted her to accept the plea bargain. The other half did not. She turned down the agreement and the preparations for trial resumed.

SELLS welcomed the positive changes resulting from his incarceration in Bexar County. He could use the telephone every day. Some of his pen pals sent their phone numbers and eagerly awaited his calls. A woman in the group turned each one into a steamy session of phone sex. After thirty days, he was allowed a television in his cell.

But there was a downside, too. "Everyone on death row knows what they are faced with. Everyone is charged with capital murder. Every one of us has a date someplace down the line for Texas to kill us," Sells said. "In San Antonio, you have some in there for jaywalking to capital murder. You have some young-ass kids think they are Mexican mafia, when all they are is a rat pack of punks."

LAW enforcement agencies continued to hound Sells for more information about old confessions and new possibilities. He told investigators in Illinois that he could take them to the gun he'd used to kill Keith Dardeen. But, in Texas, there is a law that prohibits unindicted inmates under a death sentence from leaving the state. Illinois fought that battle in court and lost.

Their effort was not ignored by the state legislature. State Representative Pete Gallego, a Democrat from Alpine in far West Texas, introduced House Bill 1472 to overturn the law. His bill was specifically designed with Tommy Lynn Sells in mind. The bill failed, mainly because of lack of support from the governor's office. The governor's policy office insisted it was necessary to keep the existing law to protect the public and the will of the State of Texas. Often, other jurisdictions want to bring prisoners to their location to testify in the trials of other defendants, or to help find evidence in open cases. The original law had been written to protect the state from the possibility that a state that does not have a death penalty would not return the inmate. Texas feared that an unindicted prisoner in one of those states could be set free or placed in a low security facility where an escape was a possibility. But, they stated, if the inmate is indicted in any other state, the governor of Texas would honor extradition papers signed by any other governor in the Union.

MORE suspicions popped up across the country. Investigators in St. Louis, Missouri, looked at Sells for three murders there in 1983. In addition to the blunt trauma deaths of 33-year-old Colleen Gill and her 4-year-old daughter, Tiffany, they also hoped he could provide details of the sexual assault and murder of an 8- to 10-year-old African-American girl. Her body was found in an abandoned building, just blocks from the Gill home on February 28. Her head was never found and her name is still not known. Sells told Texas Rangers that he'd killed a mother and child and a black female in St. Louis in two separate instances, but provided no further details. Investigators from Missouri still hoped to get something more concrete.

Outside of Houston, a woman went jogging one morning and never returned. Days later, a man driving a tractor down the road found her, her throat cut. The Texas Ranger working in that area can find no reason for the crime and has no suspects—except one possibility, Tommy Lynn Sells. Sells has vaguely alluded to committing two murders in the Houston area, but was not willing to speak to that Ranger or to provide any details about bodies resting on Texas soil.

Sergeant Buddy Cooper, with the Missouri Highway Patrol, questioned Sells about a double homicide in Portageville, a small town in the boot-heel section of the state. On March 28, 1998, Tony Scherer was out working in the fields of his farm. His wife Sherry Ann and his 12-year-old daughter, Megan, were at home. When Tony opened the door of his house, he was tempted by the tantalizing aroma of ribs being cooked for dinner. But his appetite vanished in the next moment. He saw his wife. She was naked, her belly resting on a footstool, her hands tied behind her back. Nearby, her daughter lay sprawled on the floor. Both were dead from gunshot wounds. Two hours later, investigators believed, the same man responsible for the double murder asked a Dyersburg, Tennessee, woman for directions. Then, he shot her with the same gun he'd used in Portageville. This woman later identified Tommy Lynn Sells as the man who shot her.

Sells admitted to committing these crimes. According to him, he'd knocked on the door of the farmhouse to ask for some water. The woman who answered the door was rude and disrespectful to him. He flew into a rage, killing Sherry Ann and sexually assaulting her, then murdering Megan.

Sergeant Cooper said that this case had Tommy Lynn

Sells written all over it. Sells even described a spilled anti-freeze stain on the driveway. There is just one thing that does not add up. DNA was recovered at the scene. It was not a match for Sells.

In Lawrenceville, Illinois, three years after the death of Joel Kirkpatrick, prosecutors charged Julie Rea with the murder of her son. From the start, her ex-husband, Len Kirkpatrick, reeling in grief over the loss of his son and still festering from an ugly divorce and custody battle, insisted to all who would listen that Julie was responsible.

Investigators and prosecutors were not convinced of her version of the events. Their doubts were born on many fronts. No fingerprints, DNA or other physical evidence of an intruder was recovered from the scene. From this lack, they postulated that the intruder did not exist. But Tommy Lynn Sells and others like him often walk away from a murder scene without leaving any proof of their presence behind.

Prosecutors believed that a stranger coming off the street with killing in his heart would bring a weapon. They could not accept that he could pull a knife from the kitchen drawer to use in commission of the crime. Sells did sometimes bring a weapon—sometimes he used what was at hand. Roaming the streets in October 1997 were others just like him.

Finally, prosecutors were convinced that the violence of the attack and the rage it displayed was proof that the perpetrator knew the victim. Sells demonstrated the fallacy of that logic on November 18, 1987, in Ina, Illinois.

In another major blow for the defense, Lesa Bridgett, the neighbor Julie had run to after her son's murder, testified that something indefinable about the defendant's story and demeanor was not credible.

On March 4, 2002, a jury deliberated for nearly five hours before finding Julie guilty of stabbing her son to death. On May 10, the judge sentenced her to sixty-five

years in prison. Julie Rea continued to protest her innocence.

In mid-June, 2002, Tommy Lynn Sells received a letter
that read: "The other night, I was watching a story on TV
about a woman who was in jail for killing her son. She
claims someone broke into her house and killed him. You
could say, 'Yeah right, lady. We've heard that story before.' But then you listen to the law enforcement guys and
the prosecuting attorney and they are so full of stupid opinions." The writer summarized the reasoning of the officials
and concluded, "After hearing that garbage, I believe it is
very possible that woman is telling the truth."

Sells was given no further information about the crime,
not the name of the mother or the victim, not the location
of their home, not the date the crime was committed.

In response, Sells wrote, "About that woman claims
someone broke into her house? Was that like maybe two
days before my Springfield, Mo. murder? Maybe on the
13th?"

Stephanie Mahaney was abducted from her home on
October 15, 1997. Joel Kirkpatrick was murdered on October 13, 1997.

In a subsequent letter, he wrote in reference to this
crime, "A murder don't always have to do with sex or any
of the norms y'all may want to label me with. Maybe,
someone just pissed me off and I did not want their child
to be like them. That's cold, I understand. Maybe more than
just one person is in jail for the same thing."

IT seemed for a time that Max McCoy, a reporter for *The
Joplin Globe* was the only one convinced of Sells' guilt in
the 1999 Freeman murders, the arson, and the abduction of
Ashley Freeman and Lauria Bible. Sells had told McCoy
he knew where the bodies were. To another reporter he'd
stated that he was uncertain whether he was still in
Oklahoma or across the state line in Texas when he disposed of them. Since the thought of another trial in Texas
was abhorrent to him, he refused to speak of any specifics.

At another time, he said, "About that murder up north, I'm not trying to avoid your questions about nothing. I remember something bad happened. I think I remember that lady's face. I remember small parts of what happened. But then again, there's been so many and I get mixed up with another murder. It's not that I don't want to talk about this murder or any other murder—things get real crazy inside my head."

Then, on June 17, 2002, Tommy Lynn Sells told the Texas Rangers, the Craig County Sheriff and an officer from the Oklahoma State Bureau of Investigation that he could take them to the bodies. They returned to the prison on the following Sunday with a bench warrant.

A well-guarded Sells took a field trip to locate the bodies. They headed northeast to Marshall, Texas, a town near the Louisiana border best known for its annual Fire Ant Festival and its local specialty, white clay pots. East of town, Sells identified the spot. Bones were found. But they were all cattle bones, seven to eight years old.

However, the day before this exploration, he wrote, "I know this: I'm not going to go through another trial no matter what, if I can keep from it. So if I'm not helping then it's a lot harder on them. So why do I want to cause more trouble to my life."

There are three possibilities then: either Sells is not involved in the Freeman crime; or his memory is faulty; or he intentionally took the officers to the wrong spot. A look at a road map demonstrates that en route from Welch, Oklahoma, to Del Rio, Texas, a side trip to Marshall would be a lengthy and illogical detour.

Lorene Bible, mother of Lauria, one of the missing teenagers, did not believe that Sells was responsible for the murder of the Freemans and the abduction and possible death of their daughter and her own. She still believed, though, that the crime was related to the drug business in some way. "Somebody out there knows something," she said. "There's a fifty-thousand-dollar reward—pick up the phone and call in."

Sissy, the loyal rottweiler who spent the night by Danny Freeman's side, was given to a friend of the family. She developed a bad habit of chasing chickens, and has been put to sleep.

TOMMY Lynn Sells' presence in Lockport, New York, on May 1, 1987, was certain. He told Ranger Coy Smith that he had killed a girl there. After checking with Lieutenant Richard Podgers of the Lockport Police Department, Smith learned that Susan Korcz had disappeared on that day.

Podgers pulled together a packet of photos of six different women including Susan. Then he went all around the area taking photographs—some shots were connected with the crime scene, others just scenes in the community.

Smith sat down with Sells and handed him the pictures of the women. Sells looked at them all. He dropped five photographs on the table. He held one in his hand and rubbed his thumb across the woman's face. He stared at Smith and then stared back at the photo. The snapshot he held in his fingers was that of Susan Korcz.

"What are you telling me, Tommy?" Smith asked.

Sells did not say a word. He just ran his thumb across her face again and smiled.

Smith passed the photos of the Lockport area across the table to Sells. He examined each one. Each picture that was unrelated to the crime scene, he set off to the side. When he picked up a photo connected with the incident, he'd look down at the photo, up at the Ranger, then set it down on the table directly in front of him and give it a little pat. Most telling of all was the photograph depicting the spot where Susan's body had been found. Sells' thumb unerringly landed on the exact location.

"What are you telling me, Tommy?" Smith asked again.

And again, Sells' only response was a grin.

CHAPTER THIRTY-SEVEN

SELLS returned to death row in Livingston, Texas, in time for Christmas in 2001. In his cell, he put up a Christmas tree of sorts. He used his radio for a stand. On top of the radio, there were three red and two green lights that blinked in time to the music that came through his headphone. Using his imagination, he could see a tree adorned with bright strings of lights. Beneath the tree, he laid a packet of cocoa. He drank it when he awoke on Christmas morning—his way of wishing "Merry Christmas" to Jessica, his cocoa girl.

JESSICA filed for divorce in early 2002. She resumed the identity of Jessica Levrie, her name during her previous marriage.

ALTHOUGH she has not seen him for years, Nora Sells is still married to her imprisoned husband and still as much in love with him as she was the day they married.

NINA Sells had a heart attack on the day she learned of her son's crimes. Her health has continued to deteriorate since that time. She received a phone call from the granddaughter she had never met, asking about her biological father. Nina told her that she really did not want to know. She encouraged her not to meet him, and to leave well enough alone. But Nina knows that the girl has talked to him by phone on at least one occasion. Despite her negative reaction to her granddaughter, Nina still said, "If I had the money, I'd go to see him tomorrow. He is still my son, and I love him."

SELLS' appeal on his conviction and punishment was filed in March with the Court of Criminal Appeals of the State of Texas in Austin. San Antonio attorney Mark Stevens cited thirty-eight errors in the original trial. They included three errors connected with admitting evidence over the objections of the defense, three for not entering evidence submitted by the defense, fourteen for not allowing the defendant to examine potential jurors concerning the law of parole, four other errors involved in the questioning of jurors and two for insufficient evidence. The remaining nine errors were for violations of constitutional rights and included the classic reason cited in capital murder appeals that the death penalty is cruel and unusual punishment and thus, unconstitutional under the laws of the United States and the State of Texas. The appeal ended with the request that the guilty verdict be overturned or that a new punishment phase be ordered.

FRED Hernandez won his election and became the new district attorney of Val Verde County. He requested an extension of time to file his response to the appeal.

SELLS had a lot of time to think in those long hours in his cell. He came to the conclusion that he is not a danger to society. Society is a danger to him. Out in society, the rules are always changing. In the prison, everything stayed the same. "Prison," he said, "is the only place I feel safe."

He had picked up two nicknames on death row. The Aryans call him Tommy Gun. The Mexicans call him Tom Cat. "I tell them all it's just Tommy," he said.

He also developed an explanation for why he killed children. He said he did it so they would not suffer as he had. He did it because they were being mistreated or because of the trauma they suffered by witnessing the violent death of a parent. He did it to end their unhappiness and send them to a better place.

Two psychological tests were administered to Sells in the spring of 2002: the Personality Assessment Inventory (PAI) and the Minnesota Multiphasic Inventory (MMPI). While he had the PAI in his cell, he carefully copied down all 364 questions and his answers to them. He was not up to a repeat performance on the MMPI. When that test was in his hands, he just wrote down his answers to more than 500 questions.

According to independent evaluators, his unsupervised possession of these tests for such a long period of time called their validity into question. Additionally, he gave an "all true response" on both tests. In other words, the tests showed him to have all possible psychological disorders. When this occurs, mental health professionals regard it as a cry for help. It is an indication of post-traumatic stress disorder, in all likelihood, in his case, the result of events in his childhood that have never been effectively addressed. Sells reported that he was receiving no medication or therapy for any psychological problems.

IN San Antonio, Texas, in the summer of 2002, the trial for the murder of Mary Bea Perez still awaited a date. Many attorneys and members of the law enforcement community speculated that it would never be tried in a courtroom. Then, at the end of July, a bench warrant brought Tommy Lynn Sells back to Bexar County to consult with his attorneys. The district attorney's office wanted to deal. If Sells would plead guilty to capital murder, the D.A. would not pursue the death penalty.

Sells rejected their offer and the case is expected to come to trial in the spring of 2003. The defense plans to call two alibi witnesses for the day that Mary Bea Perez was abducted and murdered. One of these witnesses is Jessica Levrie, who will testify that Sells was in Del Rio on April 18, 1999.

• • • •

SELLS was charged by the police department in Lexington, Kentucky, for the murder of Haley McHone. The case had not yet been presented to a grand jury.

Lieutenant Jimmy Hand of the Gibson County Sheriff's Department does not believe Tommy Lynn Sells is their man. He doubts his confession because Sells had no motive for the crime. In response, Sells wrote, "I can tell you from A to Z about what happened to that mother and kid and Gibson County, Tennessee, but you said they don't believe I did it. You know what I have to say. I, me, Tommy Lynn, don't have to prove I did it, they have to prove I did not do it. And they can't." The small details from that home provided by Sells have convinced the Texas Rangers of his guilt.

Detective Jeffery Stone of the Metropolitan Police Department in St. Louis, Missouri, has waited for the moment Sells will agree to talk to him about the three murders in his city. He said Sells wrote that he was reluctant to discuss those crimes because he had so many family members in the area. Stone insisted that he would not charge Sells if he is the perpetrator. He just wants to close the cases that have moldered unsolved for nearly twenty years.

LT. Larry Pope of the Val Verde County Sheriff's Department was named Texas Lawman of the Year 2001 by the Sheriffs' Association of Texas for his work in the apprehension of Tommy Lynn Sells. About his infamous prisoner he said, "Tommy doesn't get upset, ticked off and mad like everybody else does. He gets upset and he goes to murder."

SHIRLEY Timmons, once Department of Public Safety secretary, had turned her drawing hobby into a promotion to forensic artist in 1998. She was presented the Medal of Merit for the twenty-four suspects identified and nineteen arrests made with the help of her drawings over the preceding two years. Her most notable composite was the one she drew from the notes of Krystal Surles that had led to the arrest of Sells. She is only the seventeenth recipient of this honor in DPS history.

AGENT Steve Tanio with the Oklahoma Bureau of Investigation was given the 2001 Agent of the Year Award in February 2002. He was cited for his two years of intense investigation on the Bobbie Lynn Wofford homicide that resulted in a suspect and a confession. Additionally, he was noted for opening thirty-seven cases, filing fifty-two charges and performing forty polygraph investigations.

SINCE the arrest and conviction of Sells, Rangers Coy Smith and Johnny Allen have both had more than enough cases to keep them busy. Still, they can't help thinking about this one. They are haunted by the confessions that will never have resolution. The mother and child in Idaho who held up panhandling signs with Sells on the highway are still unidentified—Sells claimed he killed them and threw their bodies in the Snake River. These bodies have never been found. There was the nameless black man in Chicago whom Sells said he murdered at 48th and State Streets and then discarded in a Dumpster. Sells also bragged of bodies dumped in the alligator bayous off Interstate 10 and of a series of rest stop killings of homosexuals along the interstate in Pennsylvania. Smith and Allen badly want, but know they never will have, an accurate account of all of the victims of this one man.

In the summer of 2002, no other charges had been filed against Tommy Lynn Sells. In some cases, jurisdictions consider it a moot point.

"You can't execute the guy more than once," said Don Swan, former lead investigator in the Ena Cordt case.

IN Del Rio, Texas Rangers recovered a pair of earrings from a woman who claimed Tommy Lynn Sells had given them to her. This was the same woman who gave Sells a wedding band for Jessica when they got married. The earrings matched a necklace owned by Bobbie Lynn Wofford in Kingfisher, Oklahoma. The police, the sheriff's department and FBI agents involved in this case wanted to go to trial. But the prosecuting attorney, Ard Gates, was dragging his feet. He'd learned his caution the hard way. When he first took the job, he spent two frustrating years running down the facts in a false confession made by Henry Lee Lucas, the notorious eternal confessor in Texas. Gates did not want to be burned again.

In February 2002, Gates may have taken this determination a bit too far. He made a presentation at the local Rotary Club about the exculpatory evidence he saw in the case. He wanted to explain why he has not brought charges against Tommy Lynn Sells.

He contended, in direct contradiction to the mother of the victim, that the necklace and earrings did not match, since the two came from different manufacturers. He questioned the sincerity of the confession, since Sells would interview with OSBI Agent Steve Tanio, but not with Sheriff Graham. He also stated that he was disturbed by the lack of forensic evidence. And he suggested that the real killer could be walking the streets.

In the small town of Kingfisher, these comments were reported in the twice-weekly local, the *Kingfisher Times & Free Press*. The story ricocheted across the town faster than a Ping-Pong ball in a bingo machine.

In the next issue the following Sunday, the newspaper reported the reaction of other law enforcement officials who were disturbed that Gates had made any public comments, since all had agreed not to do so. OSBI and the sheriff's department referred to his statements as one man's opinion. Susan Wofford, the victim's mother, alleged that Gates simply does not want to prosecute because he does not support the death penalty. Gates denied her contention. Gates also came under attack for stirring up fear in the community by insinuating that a murderer was still at large.

The sheriff's department and OSBI are convinced that

Tommy Lynn Sells is their man. He'd picked Bobbie Lynn out of a photo line-up, he'd described the rural location and the route he took with her that night, he'd picked the large-caliber gun out of a line-up of different sized weapons, and they have recovered evidence from his '79 Dodge L'il Red Express. The current owner of the vehicle even confirmed the persistent slow leak in the right rear tire. Additionally, the eyewitness provided a composite of the man seen talking to Bobbie Lynn and the truck he was driving—both fit Sells and his truck. There was no evidence, however, that Bobbie Lynn had been assaulted by Sells' ratchet as he had claimed. The decomposition of her body was so advanced when she was found, that any possible evidence of this injury could have deteriorated.

IN the disappearance of Stefanie Stroh, many sources reported that the FBI no longer considered Sells a viable suspect. Of course, if they did believe his version of events, they would have to accept that they never had the authority to be involved in the case in the first place. A close friend, Caroline Waters, a Norwegian singer and performer living in Los Angeles, said that she put her faith in what has been told to her by the FBI. Additionally, Caroline said that Stefanie did not own clothing as described by Sells, and would not use drugs. But Stefanie had traveled through Europe and Asia over the preceding ten months and then embarked on a cross-country hitchhiking adventure begun in New York. Even staying at home, a 20-year-old can change a lot in a few months.

On her web site, www.carolinewaters.com, Caroline stated that she had followed up on the police investigation for four months. "I stuck my nose in everything. Found lots of dirt, corrupted police departments, among other things. I finally was told to stop playing detective, that it was too dangerous for me. I had to make a choice: Should I stay a frustrated detective, or get out there and create something?"

The result of her choice was *Compassion*, a self-produced album released in 1992 under her birth name,

Caroline Asplin. Her song, "Missing," was written in memory of Stefanie Stroh. Caroline wrote that she had composed the song as she sat in the car crying, and called it "a scream with no words."

Joni Settlemeir, Stefanie's mother, did not know what to believe. She only knew that she desperately ached for an answer to what happened to her child.

IN many other cases, like the murders of the Dardeen family, prosecutors were reluctant to bring charges and start the "speedy trial" clock running until they were certain the case was strong enough for conviction.

Along with her undying grief, Joeanne Dardeen still carried a bucketful of bitterness in 2002. She continued to feel that she had been mistreated by a long list of media outlets; but most of all, she was angry that Sells had not been captured after he murdered Ena Cordt and her son, Willie, in Gibson County, Tennessee, in 1985. If he had been, she thought, her son would be alive today. She had been living for the moment she could face Tommy Lynn Sells in the courtroom and see him prosecuted for the murder of her son, Keith, and his family in Ina, Illinois, in 1987. Law enforcement and prosecutors still struggled to find just one piece of irrefutable physical evidence that could tie Sells to the scene of the crime. If his current conviction were reversed on appeal, they, like many others, would re-evaluate their hesitation.

THE living room of John and Mary Torres, grandparents of Mary Bea Perez, was dominated by a mural of a joyful Mary Bea resting in the arms of the Virgin Mary. They visited her gravesite in San Fernando Cemetery #2 every week. Plot 4–16, in section 37, was flanked with dark pink artificial flowers in the summer of 2002. Bright yellow silk daises added an exclamation point to the end of each row. Two angels in patriotic dress bearing the slogan, "Let Freedom Ring" were planted in the ground next to her prone headstone. An American flag waved at the top, with teddy bears attached to its pole. Stuffed bears and toy dogs cavorted on top of her grave, accented by the yellow daisies. Angel figurines, colored stones and coins surrounded the inscriptions on the stone that bears the picture of Mary Bea. Visitors left behind flowers, stuffed animals and a piece of their hearts. After her death, her baby brother, Gabriel Guerrero, went to live with his father.

CRYSTAL and Terry Harris moved out to the country near Neodesha, Kansas. They continued to struggle with their emotional recovery. It took two years for them to return to church. Crystal had lost forty pounds because of her incessant need to stay busy. She said that when she's working, she doesn't think as much.

Whenever she went into town, she had a panic attack. So she spent most of her time in her house or in her wildflower garden. She missed the desert terrain of West Texas a lot, but she had brought a piece of it with her to Kansas. She'd dug up and transplanted her collection of barrel cacti. They were a lot of trouble in the cooler climate of Kansas. She had to dig them up every winter and store them indoors so that they would survive. But work was not something that Crystal avoided.

On Memorial Day, 2001, Crystal dreaded going to visit Katy's grave. "You can't hold her. You can't touch her. You're talking to a stone. It's so unfair to have to visit your child that way," she said. Still, she forced herself to fulfill an unspoken obligation. She brought flowers watered with tears and spoke to her Katy and hoped she would hear.

Later that day, a couple of friends dropped by, just passing through town. They wanted to visit Katy's plot. As much as Crystal ached at the thought of returning there on the same day, she accompanied her friends to the side of her daughter's cold grave.

Late in the afternoon, Crystal sat on the picnic bench trying to talk away her pain as Terry grilled dinner on the barbecue. Butterflies moved in slowly, one by one, until they encircled her head, fluttering around her, their wings brushing against her skin. The memory of Katy and her butterfly kisses lifted her out of her sorrow. And she knew that because she had been strong enough to visit Katy twice that day, God had allowed her to have those butterfly kisses once again.

The summer of 2002 was the happiest one for the two Harris children still living at home, 14-year-old Lori and 16-year-old Justin. Crystal had restricted their movements since that horrible night that Kaylene was murdered. She could not bear to have them out of her sight. This summer, she had forced herself to relax a bit. She still felt her fear, but allowed them a bit more freedom.

Unanswered questions still tormented Crystal. *Why did he pick us? Why did he do that to Katy? How could God let me sleep through my daughter dying?* She hushed these howling banshees with one thought: "God has a purpose in everything He does. And He knew the only way he could have been stopped was for someone to die and someone to see it and live."

PAM Surles, her daughter, Krystal, and her other girls never moved to Del Rio, Texas. They now lived in Yates Center, Oklahoma. Krystal strived to put the ordeal of that life-transforming night out of her mind. She tried to lead a normal adolescent life. But every time she glimpsed her face in a mirror or her hand grazed across her neck, the long scar was there to remind her of the nightmare she would rather forget.

TWO and a half years after the fact, Herb Betz continued to break down and cry when he talked about the night Krystal showed up on his doorstep. He imagined he always would. He and Marlene ached for news about Krystal. They had not heard from her or her mother, Pam, in more than a year.

THE families and friends of the victims have not stopped feeling their sense of loss. Some are impatient for new trials to begin; others live only for the execution of Tommy Lynn Sells.

To them, Sells simply stated, "The truth is, I've done something wrong and I'm paying for it."

AFTERWORD

"WHATEVER he does, he does for Tommy," Johnny Allen said.

"Tommy is so far past the average criminal, and I think that's what bumfuzzles so many law enforcement," Coy Smith added. "He is so far past your average criminal—not in intellect or skills, but he is so manipulative and so cunning and so far past that, people don't want to believe it. And he capitalizes on that. He capitalizes on the fact that he can tell you something, and make you believe it. Then, he can water it down or something and you question or wonder about your judgment.

"And all along while he's doing that, he knows what he's doing to you," Johnny Allen concluded.

THE following is a statement written by Tommy Lynn Sells especially for this book.

> What you have or are about to read in these pages of Ms. Fanning's book about me, I've not seen nor read. But I've made a life out of trying to read people and I believe what she has put together is as close to the truth as it will ever get about me. Not only has Ms. Fanning spent countless hours with me trying to get as much details as she can but I believe she has taken the time to get to know me. I've put trust in her only a few ever have had. If anyone has a knowledge or right to say something about me, the rage I feel toward society, or of the hate I have felt for years, from where I stand

it's Ms. Fanning. And to that, I would have to say thank you for taking the time out of your life to try and get to know the web I live in.

I will not go into trying to defend myself or my outlook, the things I've done, the pain I've caused, the emptiness I've left in people living. Only a healing can take place now or they will let an anger eat away at their lives as it has at mine.

The press news people have become my new enemy. I see them as Jews trying to mislead the truth. Harold Dow with CBS' 48 Hours asked me a question: "I've not heard you tell or give no one an apology." I tried to explain to him saying sorry doesn't work. When you do try to say it, they are always trying to show reasons why you're not. If you left a tear fall, they will try to say that tear is for himself. If I smile at a kindness that was shown to me, they will say, "See, he doesn't take nothing to heart." I tried to explain this again to Laura Bauer Menner of a newspaper in Springfield, Missouri. She tried to change what I've said as well. The truth of the matter is that sorry is just another word that I've been told all my life. It just don't work.

I don't believe that I am the same person today that I was ten years ago or five for that matter. I understand that it has come too late but I have come to believe in a higher power, a divine love. But no matter how much I try to talk of this, people want to have a one-track mind. People, "society," want to use those five-dollar words to say how bad of a person I am. But I've seen this first hand for too long. Murder is not just murder. If you are just an everyday person that works hard, pays taxes, from six to whatever, 60 years and you get killed, murder, that is all it is. Oh well. But if you're under six or a peace officer, then it's capital murder. You have just been pushed to second class because for some reason we live in a society where we put people that put their pants on one leg at a time just as we do on a pedestal. If it is supposed to be capital murder for one then it should be for all.

Capital murder means one person, in my case, Attorney for the State Fred Hernandez, gets to become "super human" to decide if you live or die. When one person has the right to make that call, that in itself is pre-meditated murder, because what he wants is to see you killed. By the laws of Texas, Mr. Hernandez would have had me dead to rights had he charged me as the crime happened. Murder, the first crime; then burglary. But, no, he wanted to super-size the case so he went with murder and sexual assault. But the truth with this is that no *evidence* leads to that outcome and because Mr. Hernandez has decided to fabricate the truth, "mislead," then he is no better than I. And if ever citizens of our society want to keep his or her rights then you will see and understand why I've let my attorneys do what they do best, stand up for our rights.

The D.A., Fred Hernandez, got his guilty verdict of my death by showing a picture of a 13-year-old girl naked on a cold stainless steel table in the morgue, her head laying on a wood block, her neck turned so the wound is open and a pair of hemostats pulling the meat of the neck back. That is what got me the guilty verdict, not evidence. I still do not get it to this day. That picture had nothing to do with what happened at the Harris home.

I am not making light of what has been done at or by my hands. Maybe John Kemp said it best, "It just goes beyond explanation so I won't try." I'll leave that for Ms. Fanning and other big wigs.

This is not about the D.A. Though I have been

condemned to die, sentence passed by a jury, not of my peers, but of his. That bunch of folks has no idea of what kind of life I've lived. I was asked not long ago was I saved. I said from what. My belief is not my religion that is for the Jews. Ask them what they did with Christ. Want to be saved from y'all till y'all kill me. I look at death as a welcome to a better life. And once again, I'm not going to get into my higher power or my beliefs. It would just leave another door opened for a Jew to kick at. I do believe my life will be much better on the other side. I am an orphan child. I am my strength. I believe in the law of nature. That would be my spiritual heritage. The Lord is my friend. I've found him before the end.

As the others, I want to cry and scream. Our hearts burst with sadness and sorrow. The pain I've taken in and given is a darkness I've been terrified of almost as long as I can remember. This is not just in my head but throughout my body. I guess a few has been worrying about me but to them I say I'm ready. I'm tired of the pain and feel it all the time. I'm tired of being alone. I never knew where I was going or where I just came from. I'm tired of people being mean to each other. I've just not known how to help. The darkness is my greatest fear. I'm all broken up on the inside. That's how it is everyday all over.

I hope all can forgive me. Don't let that rage and hate keep eating at you as it has me. It will destroy you.

Jessica, you and yours really tried. Y'all was able to open a door with me no one else had up to that point in time. If I was ever able to love, it was by you. It just came a little late.

Donna, you have opened my eyes to so many things. If anyone can understand me, it's you.

My family: I love y'all.

My Del Rio attorney, Victor Garcia, first ever Mexican Jew I met. But because you are a Mexican, I guess you tried. You should have had help!

San Antonio Attorneys Jay Norton, "Jew," Michael McCrum, want to be Jew, Susan Reed, D.A., Ha, Ha, Fuck y'all.

Texas Rangers John W. Allen, Coy L. Smith. Someone had to do it.

Sheriff A. D'Wayne Jernigan Isaiah 55:7.

Lt. Larry Pope. It takes one to understand one.

Tony. Miss you.

Texas Death Row. Inhuman, cruel act on humans. Out of all my rage, I've never once made one of my victims suffer as y'all do. I want the Texas Department of Criminal Justice to explain how y'all have come up with a way to discipline: loss of privilege, either food, gas, commissary, visits, along with other means. Brute force can rehabilitate a person? So what y'all are doing here on death row is an act of revenge.

Again, the jury was not told everything. But not telling the whole truth is just as bad as lying. I am controlled in this society 100% on Death Row. Is this society safe for us?

TDCJ Ad-Seg does have a plan to control all convicts. Spokesperson for TDCJ, Royce Smithey, chief investigator, said at my trial if you put a person on death row and execute them, I guarantee you they won't be violent. Maybe he should guarantee to every person in society that brute force is the key to their safety. Might is right. Death is the key to getting rid of something. The only contact I have with anyone in this society is when I stick my hands behind my back through a bean hole. I was overlooked as a child.

I am overlooked again by truth and justice.

I'm a one-man band. Don't hold nothing against my family, friends or loved ones. They are

just doing what y'all are doing: trying to cope with
it all.

    Ms. Fanning. Thank you.

Peace,
Tommy Lynn Sells 999367
Death Row
3872 FM 350 South
Livingston, Texas 77351

It is easy to look at crimes committed by Tommy Lynn
Sells and say, "There is a monster." The problem is far
more complex than that. Yes, Sells has done many evil
things. But it is dangerous to polarize him or those like him
and see nothing in them but bad. Individuals with anti-
social personality disorder are often very charming and
likeable in the right setting. If you are only prepared for a
one-dimensional monster, they will catch you off guard.

It is difficult for the average person to comprehend the
existence of a killer so cold-blooded he is capable of beat-
ing to death a newborn baby seconds after her birth. It is
impossible to understand.

We naturally find it repugnant for a person who commits acts like these to be included in the group we call our
fellow human beings. But he is.

He has his own set of moral guidelines that intersect
our own in some places. The most obvious example was
during the flood, when he tried to rescue a woman as she
was washed down the street, and when he tried to free a
trapped cat under the house.

Then, there are areas in his code of behavior that travel
over very alien ground. In the murder of Haley McHone,
for example, he blamed the neighborhood. He said that they
knew the overgrown area was dangerous. The body of a
college student had been left back there only a year and a
half before. He said that, had they cleaned up that area after
that murder, if they had thought first of the safety of their
children, he would never have had an opportunity to kill
that girl. He pointed a righteous finger at community neg-

ligence rather than carrying the weight of the blame on his own shoulders.

Many people who encountered Tommy Lynn Sells were surprised to find a charming, enjoyable conversationalist—from hardened investigators to Crystal Harris, who felt betrayed by her own ability to judge people. She described the man she knew before the crime as "a young man who came to us for help and guidance."

Beneath Sells' glib charm is a rotted treasure chest brimming with manipulative cunning, barely suppressed anger and an abiding sense that everyone is out to get him, so he'd better get his licks in first.

Whenever we look at someone like Tommy Lynn Sells, we are left with the big question of Why? Textbooks are full of possible explanations. Anti-social personality disorder is created in a stew of childhood violence and abuse, early maternal rejection and organic brain damage. There are others who have passed through these tortures and, although wounded, did not take the same path as Sells.

Ultimately, there are a lot of unknowns with this disorder. Likely it is the cumulative effect of these factors and more that have yet been identified, but which together simmer in young developing minds, warping their thought processes and producing violent perpetrators.

These are people who are easily bored, but not readily aroused. What would excite one of us would leave a psychopath untouched. Once they cross the line and commit their first murder, a barrier is broken and they are compelled to commit these violent acts again and again. They get immediate gratification and release, but never find a level of permanent satisfaction.

In interviewing and researching Sells, I became familiar with many aspects of his personality, but not one side of him seemed to have reality as a touchstone.

I saw a man who dearly loved his last wife, Jessica, and who had bonded with her two sons. One who still loved his mother despite their unhappy past—someone who wanted to understand why every relationship he ever had had ended in abandonment.

I also saw a person who could lie and, at the moment of his deceit, truly believe he was telling the truth—one whose self-aggrandizement surpassed the rantings of a young Muhammad Ali, and whose tricks of manipulation spooled off his tongue without conscious thought.

Then, there was the little boy. The one who yearned for love and family. The one who still had pleasant dreams of the carousel birthday cake his Aunt Bonnie made for him, and who still had nightmares about the man who sexually assaulted him with regularity when he was a child.

Finally, I saw the sharp up-ticks of anger, the flared eyes, the clenched fists, the pinched lips that heralded the arrival of the predator. Then I would be looking at a killer capable of throttling a girl for five eternally long minutes while her life slowly fled into the night; a murderer willing to beat a woman or a child to death with a bat; an unbridled aggressor who could slice a throat without a twinkling of remorse.

My method of coping with this waltz with evil was to create a Janus-like figure in my head. One face was the Tommy who made me laugh—on the other side, the face that made me cringe in fear. This separation, too, is a form of the polarization that mental health professionals decry. But for me, walking down the dark corridor of Sells' life, it was my shield.

Tommy Lynn Sells is behind bars, locked securely on death row, awaiting his execution. We are now all safe from him—but, unfortunately, he is not an anomaly.

"I have never, never met anybody that's as manipulative. Most of the time when you talk to someone who's done something wrong, it's almost like they have a sense of remorse or regret. He just likes to keep killing from beyond the grave. He can just manipulate you and there's nothing you can do about it," said Texas Ranger Coy Smith.

Ranger John Allen added, "This guy went eighteen

years killing people and never, never got caught. How did he do that? He was never even a suspect. If he never mouthed off, he would never be a suspect in one other homicide—anywhere. That's what blows my mind."

UPDATE

ON September 11, 2003, Sells entered District Judge Pat Priest's courtroom in San Antonio and pled guilty to the murder of nine-year-old Mary Bea Perez. He confessed to abducting her from a festival in downtown San Antonio and assaulting her on a filthy mattress in a nearby field. The little girl begged for her life: "Please don't hurt me no more."

"That's when I choked her," Sells confessed. "Dead man leaves no tales."

In a plea agreement, the judge sentenced Sells to life in prison, in addition to his current death sentence.

The following week, a grand jury in Greene County, Missouri, returned a first-degree murder indictment for Sells in the death of 13-year-old Stephanie Mahaney. Authorities sent a warrant for his arrest to Texas but had no plans to request custody of him until all his appeals in the Del Rio case were exhausted.

In June 2005, Chief Neil Merritt announced that the Lockport, New York, police were closing the books on the May 1987 murder of 27-year-old Suzanne Korcz. Although New York authorities were convinced of Sells's guilt, they had no plans to extradite him for trial since he was already on death row.

THE first edition of this book served as a catalyst for the most dramatic development in the investigation of Sells's life and crimes. Prior to the book's publication in April 2003, Julie Rea Harper had been sitting in Dwight Correctional Center serving a 65-year sentence for the murder of her son, Joel Kirkpatrick. Julie's family, the Downstate Illinois Innocence Project at the University of Illinois at Springfield, and Julie's appeals attorney, Robert Bunting, then read *Through the Window*, including Sells's confession to that murder.

In July 2003, Bill Clutter, an Innocence Project investigator, found witnesses in Lawrenceville, Illinois, who reported seeing a stranger in town behaving unusually on the weekend of Joel's murder. The sheriff's department had ignored them, not taking formal statements or investigating their stories at all.

Julie's defense decided to request DNA tests, and after intense media coverage and courtroom negotiations, the state finally relented. In early September, the legal team headed by Bunting argued before the Illinois Court of Appeals for the overturn of Julie's conviction based on existing evidence. Then they awaited the ruling of the court.

In the meantime, the Innocence Project presented a case to the Illinois Prison Review Board on October 24, requesting executive clemency for Julie: "One cannot begin to imagine the horror of losing a precious 10-year-old boy to a cold-blooded sociopathic serial killer. But to suffer the blows of the accusation that was leveled against her—persecuted and victimized by a criminal justice system that has demonstrated a miserable track record for getting it wrong—is the ultimate act of injustice." The board took no action.

In the months to come, Sells answered questions posed by authorities, the media, and Julie's new champions, the Center for Wrongful Convictions at Northwest University. Throughout, the salient aspects of his confession remained unchanged.

Karen Daniel and Judith Royal, attorneys with the Center, outlined the facts pointing to Sells's guilt and submitted a petition for relief from judgment. Included in their arguments was an affidavit from retired Texas Ranger John Allen, the foremost expert on Sells's murders, stating that in his professional opinion, Sells's confession and the corroborating evidence were "compelling evidence of his guilt."

On June 25, 2004, the court issued its ruling: Julie's conviction was overturned on a technical point of law. Two weeks later, at Dwight Correction Center, Julie's family and friends prepared to be reunited with her. To their horror, Julie emerged in handcuffs, in the custody of Lawrence County authorities who had, once again, charged her with the murder of her son.

After legal wrangling over bail and an outpouring of donations from across the country, Julie, at last, gained her freedom on bond one month after her conviction was overturned. Almost two years later in March of 2006, the judge ruled that the evidence regarding Sells's responsibility for Joel's murder was admissible in court.

Julie walked into the courtroom for her second trial in July. After twelve hours of jury deliberation, she stood rigid by her lead trial attorney Ron Safer and watched the jurors file in for the moment of truth.

The verdict echoed in the quiet chamber: "Not guilty." Julie cried out and fell to the floor.

Despite the decision—despite overwhelming evidence in support of the jury's conclusion—the state stubbornly clung to their belief in Julie's guilt. They would not admit to any possibility of error. They refused to reopen the case and investigate the responsibility of any other perpetrator in the murder of Joel, their ears deaf to his continued cry for justice.

SELLS has a new woman in his life—Victoria Lynn Zubcic of Lonedell, Missouri, who operates a bail bond company in the nearby town of Union. Sells refers to her as his fiancée. With Vicky's help, Sells finally terminated his opportunistic marriage to Nora Price. The divorce papers arrived in his cell on his 42nd birthday—June 28, 2006. Polk County, Texas, issued a marriage license for the couple on November 3.

* * *

SELLS'S direct appeal to have his conviction overturned made its way to the United States Supreme Court without success. The second and final appeal under the Texas death penalty statute, the habeas writ, alleged that the court-appointed attorney, Victor Garcia, and mitigation specialist, Vince Gonzales, accepted $5,000 for providing information about a double murder in Taney County, Missouri—paid by an official in that state—and that they failed to properly investigate Sells's background for mitigating evidence of mental illness, organic brain damage, or traumatic sexual abuse as a child. Sells's attorney, Terry MacDonald, also charged Garcia with conflict of interest. He claimed that Garcia's pursuit of book rights and television interviews gave Garcia a vested interest in his client's conviction—that the story had more value if Sells received a death sentence. The appeal was denied by the State of Texas appeals process.

In January 2006, authorities in Texas transported Sells from death row in Livingston to his original trial court venue in Del Rio—a journey of more than 400 miles—to receive his assigned death date. The court ordered his execution for May 17, 2006.

But in mid-March, Sells received a stay of execution— a temporary reprieve to allow him to appeal in federal court. San Antonio Attorney Alan Futrell filed the petition for writ of habeas corpus in the United States Western District Court in Del Rio on August 17. The first of the seventeen claims in the document stated that Sells was ineligible for execution because he is mentally retarded. The next week, Futrell submitted a request for a stay because the state court had not yet ruled on the mental retardation issue. Many who have spent time with Sells found that claim laughable. Nonetheless, the request was granted.

Sells said that his lawyer predicts he will face execution by lethal injection in late 2007 or early 2008.